40 *Engaging* BRAIN-BASED

TOOLS FOR THE CLASSROOM

40 Engaging BRAIN-BASED

TOOLS FOR THE CLASSROOM

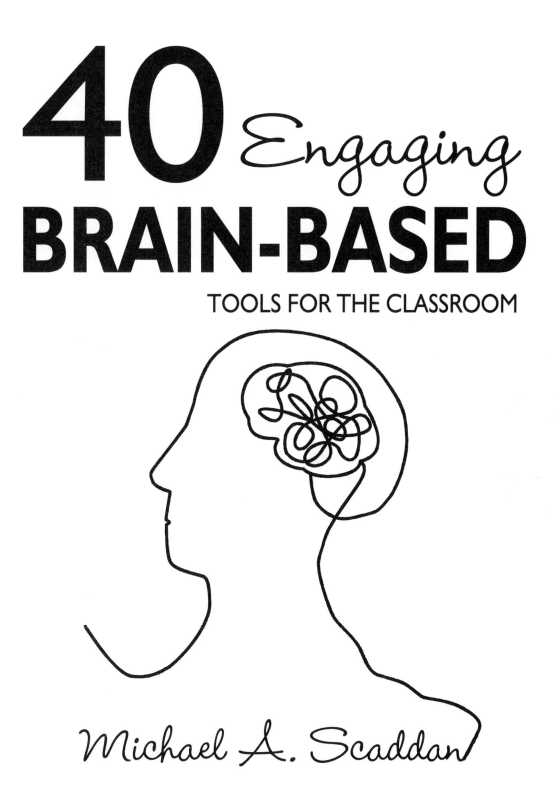

Michael A. Scaddan

CORWIN PRESS

A SAGE Company

For information:

Corwin Press
A SAGE Company
2455 Teller Road
Thousand Oaks, California 91320
www.corwinpress.com

SAGE Ltd.
1 Oliver's Yard
55 City Road
London EC1Y 1SP
United Kingdom

SAGE Pvt. Ltd.
B 1/I 1 Mohan Cooperative Industrial Area
Mathura Road, New Delhi 110 044
India

SAGE Asia-Pacific Pte. Ltd.
33 Pekin Street #02-01
Far East Square
Singapore 048763

Printed in the United States of America.

Library of Congress Cataloging-in-Publication Data

Scaddan, Michael A.
40 engaging brain-based tools for the classroom/Michael A. Scaddan.
     p. cm.
Includes bibliographical references and index.
ISBN 978-1-4129-4913-2 (cloth)
ISBN 978-1-4129-4914-9 (pbk.)
   1. Learning, Psychology of. 2. Teaching—Psychological aspects. 3. Learning strategies.
4. Brain. I. Title. II. Title: 40 engaging brain-based tools for the classroom.

LB1060.S33 2009
370.15—dc22   2008019168

This book is printed on acid-free paper.

08   09   10   11   12   10   9   8   7   6   5   4   3   2   1

Acquisitions Editors:	Allyson P. Sharp, Carol Chambers Collins
Editorial Assistants:	David Andrew Gray, Brett Ory
Production Editor:	Veronica Stapleton
Copy Editor:	Lori Wingate
Typesetter:	C&M Digitals (P) Ltd.
Proofreader:	Sue Irwin
Indexer:	Sheila Bodell
Cover Designer:	Lisa Riley

Contents

Acknowledgments

Thanks to all the staff and students at Te Puna School who have helped to make this journey of brain-compatible learning so meaningful.

Corwin Press thanks the following reviewers for their contributions to this work:

Dr. Barrie Bennett
Professor of Professional Learning & Development:
    Roles of Knowledge Creation
The University of Toronto
Ontario, Canada

Joan Cundiff
Gifted Education Coordinator
Intermediate School District, #287
Plymouth, MN

Sheryl Feinstein, EdD
Professor of Secondary Education
Augustana College
Sioux Falls, SD

Tara McGuigan
Science Teacher and GATE Resource Teacher
Madison High School
San Diego, CA

Bob Nelson, EdD
Instructor of Advanced Teacher Education
University of Texas at Dallas
Dallas, TX

About the Author

Michael A. Scaddan is not only a successful and innovative professional trainer, he has also led a highly successful school down the path of brain-compatible learning. As a principal, he continues to be a practical, hands-on educator, teaching all grade levels of students on a regular basis. This enables him to acquire and develop hundreds of useful and practical classroom tips as well as fine tune the successful schoolwide techniques that he passes on to fellow educators.

Always looking for a better way, he has extensive training in brain-compatible learning. He completed a Masters of Education in accelerated learning and gained certification as a trainer with the Jensen Corporation.

Currently Michael offers more than 20 one- to three-day workshops on a wide range of learning topics.

He now works as a fulltime learning consultant in the USA, Sweden, Hungary, Singapore, Australia, and New Zealand, and has been an educational consultant to the government of Thailand.

The author can be reached at scaddan.mike@gmail.com.

Introduction

So much of what we do as teachers is intuitive, based on our own unique communication style and a lifetime of experiences. Although our teaching may be successful, sharing and explaining why it works is often difficult. This is especially so with the subtle techniques that we use nonconsciously. I found this out early in my career—I knew what succeeded but didn't really understand why.

In 1995, I became principal of Te Puna School in New Zealand, and as a staff, we began the journey that I had personally committed to a few years before: a journey of brain-compatible learning. Put simply, this meant investigating the best learning research from behaviorists, neuroscientists, and cognitive (learning/thinking) researchers and then putting what worked best into a holistic school program. It not only provided a "why" for much of our current practice, it also extended our teaching, often in subtle yet powerful ways.

Through this understanding, the staff was able to discuss what they did and why it worked with other educationalists, parents, and most important, with students. The approach saw substantial gains in achievement and a radical improvement in behavior.

I believe that a brain-compatible approach is needed in our schools. We are all faced with continual rapid change. For a variety of reasons, the learners with whom we work today are different. They are encountering and working through many issues, including changes in the family and the influence of technology through all facets of life. The expectations for teachers and how they are viewed by society has also changed, whether we like them or not.

In many cases, traditional methods—referred to by some educators as the "factory model"—are no longer working as effectively as they used to. If we want success for learners, we need to understand people rather than content, emotions rather than test results, learning rather than teaching. In short, we need a broader range of skills and an understanding of how our brain, mind, and body function in the learning situation.

That's why I wrote this book. It is a compilation of many of the brain-compatible techniques that we read about at our school and found so successful. Whether you are new to this style of learning or an old hand, I'm sure that you will find these tools useful. Remember to modify them as necessary for your own unique environment.

SUGGESTIONS FOR USING THIS BOOK

The ideas in this book are based upon practical classroom ideas. Although I have included research or theoretical references for most ideas, space dictated that elaboration of this research was not possible. There are many other books that are excellent sources in this regard. I have included an extensive bibliography for those who wish to read further.

The book is designed so that the classroom teacher can practice a series of practical tips every week of the year. The book is set out in four parts, each divided into ten chapters presenting ten tools. They are all practical tips and have been tried and tested in classrooms spanning a variety of ages and cultural groups.

I have begun with an emphasis on that all-important issue: relationships. These are followed by issues of memory and concentration, because these are so important to help us achieve understanding. The third part helps students find out how they learn so that they can begin to take ownership of their own life and learning. I have left it until this time so that the teacher will feel more confident in their ability to "let go" and also because by this stage of the year, the students should feel more secure in their ability to take learning risks. The final part deals with specific teaching techniques. More experienced teachers may want to read Part IV earlier.

Once introduced, the tools are designed to be used continually and in a variety of ways according to your needs and experience. For the beginner, I recommend that you introduce them sequentially, one tool per week; with experience, they may be selected as needed. As you progress, you may want to introduce more than one tool at a time in a parallel process.

The overview on the following pages shows how the brain-compatible philosophy developed at Te Puna School. The "I care" philosophy is the umbrella under which we operate. The factors included under the "I care" umbrella make up our own unique model. For your school community to succeed, you will need to develop your own philosophy that is unique to your own needs. If you have not already done this, it is an important place to begin. It may develop as you read this book, but it must work for you.

I believe that any philosophy must be based around people. The idea that technology will save the world and education is, in my view, false. It is people using technology and moving through the issues that it creates that will make the difference. Understanding people is where education is. Understanding yourself is where it all begins.

MODEL

I hope that reading this book will be part of your personal journey and will inspire you to explore what you think about and stand for as an educator. It is only through the process of constant questioning and reflection that we move forward. Finally, think about your school—what is your philosophy? What is your school's philosophy? Our school's philosophy for brain-compatible learning represents the big picture of how brain-compatible learning developed at Te Puna School.

**One School's Model of
Brain-Compatible Learning**

I CARE PHILOSOPHY

Based on understanding of uniqueness and need for security

Interwoven through

THEMES

Incorporating

SHARED VALUES   HIGH LEVEL THINKING   EQ   PROBLEM SOLVING

Developing dependence to independence to interdependence
Units of work become the vehicle to teach and learn in
a brain-compatible manner

Delivered through   Processed and reinforced using
LEARNING STYLES   **QUALITY PRACTICE**

Learning demonstrated and assessed via
MULTIPLE INTELLIGENCES

Reinforced through
TEACHER MODELING   and   SENSORY EXPERIENCES

Retained in long-term memory through
REGULAR USAGE   and   REVIEW and REFLECTION

Transferred using
SERVICE TO COMMUNITY   and   REAL LIFE APPLICATION

Leading to
DEVELOPING UNDERSTANDING   and   SKILLS TO MANAGE SELF

and

Contributing to the world.

- The "I care" philosophy is the umbrella for the culture of the school. It has four statements. "I care for myself, I care for others, I care for property, and I care for the environment." These statements became the core guide when dealing with students over any issue.
- Themes are the abstract ideas that bind the teaching program together. They are big-picture issues on which to base units of work.
- Higher-level thinking skills, emotional intelligence (EQ) factors, and issues relating to moral intelligence—empathy, conscience, self-control, respect, kindness, tolerance, and fairness—are woven into the themes as life skills.
- Teaching units are then delivered, taking into account learning styles. Here, choice and variety are paramount.
- The processing occurs through the five memory pathways: semantic, episodic, procedural, conditioned response, and emotional.
- Learning can be presented, demonstrated, and assessed through different forms of intelligence.
- Learning is reinforced through the senses, both consciously and nonconsciously. The teacher needs to be aware of the hidden curriculum, especially cultural and gender biases. Reinforcement occurs through modeling, displays of posters and completed work, affirming messages, and through a variety of sensory experiences.
- Finally, if it is worth learning, it is worth retaining. This is done by having a real-life application for the learning, as well as regular usage. The brain works on a "use it or lose it" principle, so if it is not given regular practical application the learning is lost. This process is known as review.

The forty tools show how this model is put into practice.

PART I

Enhancing Relationships

1

Emotional Links

In her book *Mapping the Mind*, Rita Carter (1998) states that the teaching and learning process is all about relationships. In fact, unless this emotional engagement is made, learning will not "stick" positively in the memory (Goleman, 1996; Jensen, 2005; LeDoux, 1996).

In order to form a relationship, clear ground rules need to be established (Prentice, 2007). Because the teacher is the adult, this is the teacher's responsibility. However, with the emphasis on coverage of content, it can happen that these social expectations are never clearly shared with students.

Part of the development of these expectations is sharing appropriate information about yourself. You may share about your family, your interests, and your ambitions, but this is not enough.

More important is to share with them what you believe in.

This then provides a knowledge base as to the "life rules" that you live by and expect in the classroom setting (Borba, 2001). Sharing your own thoughts and dreams develops a model of trust (DePorter, Reardon, & Singer-Nourie, 1999), which in turn gives students the opportunity to do the same. Use these exercises to open the lines of communication between you and your students.

WHAT I'LL DO FOR YOU AND WHAT I'LL NEVER DO FOR YOU

Share clear statements so that learners will form an understanding of what drives you, your passions, and your purpose as a teacher. These are some examples:

- "I will help you with your learning by providing interesting experiences and opportunities for you to explore. I will never do your thinking for you."
- "I will support you through any problems that you encounter to the best of my ability; however, I cannot support you completely if you lie or fail to reveal the whole truth to me."

- "I will offer you options and choices; however, if the situation involves risk or danger, I will make the final choice as to what happens."

"YOU DON'T KNOW THIS ABOUT ME BUT . . ."

This is an opportunity for both you and the students to share things about yourselves: Where you were born, how many brothers and sisters you have, your ambitions, mistakes that you have made, and what you have learned from them. Some discretion may be required in this area. This process could involve one person per day or could be completed in groups using a talking circle process.

VIP CENTER

A display area is set up and the person selected to be VIP brings a "treasure" from home every day for a week. These may include photos, certificates, awards, or mementos. The VIP then makes a presentation to the class.

In my experience, five- to seven-year-olds will need to talk about their center every day. Eight- to ten-year-olds can present at the end of the week, whereas I found that it worked best for eleven- to thirteen-year-olds if they began their display on a Tuesday and presented the following Monday. Remember that for most of these senior students, there was a clear understanding of the process through years of experience. Now was the time to expand it. This inclusion of a weekend gave them time to practice presentation techniques and involve IT/PowerPoint/video processes or other props so that it was not only about themselves, it also developed life skills.

This process could involve self/peer/teacher evaluation, but this is not necessary. I have also seen it involve a child-portrait artist who presented the portrait and a summary of the presentation to the VIP. There may also be a requirement to discuss and involve family members. In fact, parents regularly turned up for these presentations, and one parent wrote a fabulous reference for her child and read it to him as part of the presentation day.

Choosing the VIP is best done on a weekly basis with the name drawn out of a hat by the previous presenter. This helps to maintain anticipation and ensures that all students have a turn. The activity can be completed with the award of a certificate with attributes contributed by classmates written on it.

Humans are the only living creatures that try to live independently.

Nature operates through interdependence.

It was near the end of the school year when I was privileged to be part of an emotional unburdening. A very shy senior student who would rarely speak in front of the class had her week as the VIP. It was day five of her special week, the day to present to her peers. She stood nervously in front of the class, head down, feet scuffing the floor. We waited in silence for what seemed minutes willing her to have the courage to begin. Two or three false starts intensified the mood. Finally, after a deep and quivering breath and with her head down she began to speak.

(Continued)

(Continued)

"You may not know that I live with my Auntie and Uncle." Long pause. "That is because my parents didn't treat me very well so I was taken away from them." She then began to tell us some of the tragic moments of her short life and how wonderful it was to be part of a new family. A family, short on money, but large on love. During the entire story her head remained down and her voice shaky and quiet. That was until she reached the end when for the first time she looked up and with a tiny smile said, "Thank you."

I looked at the class teacher who had very wet eyes which mirrored my own. The class was silent as many of the students, aged twelve and thirteen, wiped away their tears as the girl quietly returned to her seat. It was a privilege to be part of the process.

I was also present at a VIP presentation when a very different story occurred. Again it concerned a senior student's presentation, a thirteen-year-old boy who began to speak to the class. Just as his presentation began, his mother entered the room. She quietly listened as he proudly told the class about his family and some of his life's achievements sharing photos and certificates. At the conclusion of his presentation, his mother then moved to the front of the room with a piece of paper. She introduced herself explaining that what she was about to read was a reference that she had written for her son. "To whom it may concern. You may not know my son as well as I do, so I wish to share some of his attributes." She then proceeded to read about what a fine young man he was and how he made his family proud. Two VIPs. Two special emotional links for all concerned.

SOURCE: Michael A. Scaddan

2

Metaphors

Metaphors and personal stories about life are a great way to establish emotional links and reinforce the values that you want to create in your classroom (Gelb, 1995; Owen, 2001; Tate, 2004).

Powerful stories operate at the conscious and nonconscious level, challenging or confirming thoughts (Levin, 2003; Sharma, 2006). The brain is a meaning-making organ, so stories, followed at times by discussion, enhance this process. Stories told vividly can transport us from the classroom to another place and time. Remember also that in this age of virtual reality, stories are a refreshing experience (Carr, 1998).

GUIDELINES FOR STORYTELLING

- Tell the story rather than reading it. For this to be effective, you may need to practice. Try it out at home. Placing cushions wearing hats or sunglasses on the couch as your audience can be helpful.
- Avoid retelling it word for word. Perfection is not the goal. Instead, the aim is a living story. Practice linking key concepts and put your own personality into it.
- Simple props and the use of accents can help, however overuse can detract from the message.
- Have students move from their desks to a storytelling area, preferably a space in the classroom where they can sit on the floor to listen. Some storytellers sit on a stool or cushion. This all helps to create an atmosphere of expectation.
- Sometimes the students may sit in a way that makes them part of the story. For example, they could form three sides of a square that could be the walls of a house, with you as the fourth wall.

- They may also have a role in the story, repeating a chorus statement or manipulating certain props.
- Vary your pace, your tone, and your tempo. This is vital. At times you may bend forward and whisper and at other times shout to emphasize a point and to change the listener's state.
- Use your hands and body to create the scene. You **will** need to move in some form.
- Some stories may need discussion because deeper meanings may be obscure. Rather than simply telling, use discussion and higher-level questions to reveal possibilities (see Tool 37). At other times, have a clear, simple message.
- Try to have a different story each week to promote an idea. Books such as *Chicken Soup for the Soul* (Canfield & Hansen, 2003) are great sources of material.

STORIES HAVE A VARIETY OF USES

- as a state-change to alter the mood or energy level of the group
- to reframe a problem or see it from another point of view
- to challenge unacceptable behavior
- to teach a point indirectly
- to demonstrate the power of creative thinking
- as an open loop that can be closed at a later date, thereby heightening expectation
- to create associations
- to demonstrate relationships
- to shift a paradigm
- to surprise or entertain
- to illustrate a point
- to encourage a love of culture and oral tradition
- to promote genre writing

There are some wonderful stories about famous people and their experiences of initial rejection and hardship. These include Winston Churchill, Fred Astaire, and Walt Disney.

Metaphors are other people's stories about your life.

3

Rules, Guidelines, and Agreements

RULES

Many classes and schools are run on a framework of rules. Rules are not negotiable, and if they are your only framework, results and learning will be limited (Glasser, 1998; Kohn, 1996).

Rules are often based on three false assumptions.

The first is that anybody could master and control from the top, the dynamic and ever-changing system we call a classroom. The second assumption is that giving orders and being in control is the same thing. Finally, some educators falsely assume that a tightly disciplined class is a place where positive learning can take place.

Rules are defined as the imposition of authority (Glasser, 1992). They do have a place but should only be there to cover situations where a swift response is needed. These would include important safety issues, such as physical assault, intentional property damage, and substance abuse, and personal property issues, such as theft.

Rules are for everyone and are not negotiable.

GUIDELINES

A guideline is more of an indication as to what is expected (Kohn, 1996). Guidelines might relate to manners, noise level in the classroom, and the method used for formal discussion. In this sense they are relationship-based.

AGREEMENTS

In *Tribes*, Jeanne Gibbs (1995) defines an agreement as an opportunity to build relationships and responsibility. Agreements are generally process-related. They may relate to seating arrangements, a behavior code, or "home learning" expectations. (*Home learning* is a term we invented at Te Puna School, as it sounded more positive and was more specific in intent than the usual term *homework*). These agreements involve rights and responsibilities (Rief & Heimburge, 1996).

> *A class runs best and learners are much more motivated when they have a degree of control in their own destiny.*

The process of setting limits and successfully working within them gives a student a sense of structure and stability. This process is what is advantageous about agreements.

Agreements need discussion, they need thinking about, and they involve a degree of self-discipline (Kohn, 1996). Remember that the teacher and students reserve the right to revisit the agreements and amend as necessary. This is comparable to the constitutional changes that a formal institution regularly undergoes to adapt to problems.

Formalize each agreement with a vote. Voting is usually a simple for-or-against process; however this approach can be flawed because it is too limited regarding options. Much of the voting is also dependent on peer pressure.

Instead, use the voting process as an opportunity to promote higher-level thinking. Each student votes on a scale of one to five.

- 5: I fully agree with the proposal.
- 4: It is a good idea.
- 3: I can live with it.
- 2: I have some reservations.
- 1: I strongly oppose it.

The teacher then asks the *1* voters what amendments need to be made to the proposal for them to change their vote to at least a *3*. Discussion takes place and a decision is made. This process helps prevent sabotage by those who are definitely against the agreement, and it is democracy in action (Kaufeldt, 2001).

Following these procedures allows the teacher to be an influencer rather than a controller. The control process often becomes a constant tug-of-war that results in everyone being a loser because the reason for being there, positive learning, is lost. The teacher who understands influence understands the "ripple effect." This teacher focuses on continual development of his or her own behavior and uses that as a model to help up-skill others.

> *Giving orders and being in control are not the same thing.*

4

Choice

In his book *Choice Theory*, William Glasser (1998) emphasizes that choice is a critical ingredient in maintaining learner motivation. It literally alters the chemistry in the brain by lowering stress levels. Increasing positive feelings about the task promotes the production of dopamine and serotonin, two powerful neurotransmitters (Dennett, 1996; Jensen, 2006; Kovalik, 1997; Robertson, 1999). These increase our feelings of confidence and ultimately our ability to complete a task successfully (Fogarty, 2002).

The amount of choice given will vary with the activity and the age of the learner. Generally too much choice can have the same effect as too little: an increase in stress (Howard, 2000).

With too much choice, learners will return to the safe known path.
Too little, and the passion needed for learning may be stifled.

Choice needs to be introduced slowly and within a clear framework so that learners are comfortable with the process (DePorter, 1999).

To begin, provide choice on small things. The following statements are examples of how to offer limited choices:

- "Please complete questions one and two on this worksheet and at least two other questions."
- "When you receive your test, you may answer the questions in any order."
- "For this task you may work on your own, with a partner, or in threes."
- "There are six sections in this study. Begin with your title page, and then arrange the six in the order that is most suitable for you."
- "From the list provided, decide the best way for you to assess your work. If you have any other ideas, please see me."

Use phrases such as these:

- "You may decide to . . . ."
- "Another way of trying this could be . . . ."
- "Some people have found that . . . ."

Choice is a major part of the goal-setting process. This is what stimulates the important "what's in it for me" process (Kraus, 2002). Once the learner becomes more confident about making choices, personal understanding can grow. Now the learner will be more able to set goals in areas of personal, physical, social, and academic endeavor (Glasser, 1998).

It is important that the learners understand that
all choices involve consequences.

Some choices will be more positive, while others more negative. (I refer to these, especially with boys, as "winning choices" or "losing choices"). However, it is important that the learner have the right, within reason, to make these choices. This is what life is all about.

As part of this process, learners need to experience what it is like to lose. Some in society would like to protect children from the experience of losing by removing competition, but experiencing both winning and losing is important for personal growth so that we can then develop strategies to deal with both issues. Playing simple board games, such as Snakes and Ladders/Chutes and Ladders, are good for this purpose.

The more students take ownership of their own learning,
the more they are likely to develop intrinsic motivation.

5

Stress Reduction

Anything a learner perceives as stressful is!

The human brain's prime purpose is survival, the secondary purpose is meeting emotional needs, and the third is cognitive learning (Carter, 1998). Although some stress is necessary in the classroom as a motivator, only when high stress is minimized will the brain allow cognitive learning to take place (Dispenza, 2007; Howard, 2000).

High stress is a barrier to learning. It sends signals to the amygdala, the "flight and fight" response center in the brain, and reduces flow to the thalamus, which receives input from all senses except smell (Howard, 2000; Kutolak, 1997).

Stress reduces blood flow to the prefrontal cortex, the center for common sense and decision making (Jensen, 2006; Sapolsky, 1998). This is why the response to stress is not logical; it is emotionally based. It is also why asking a stressed person why she behaved in a certain way will often get an inadequate response. She probably doesn't know why. As far as she knows, the reaction just happened.

The negative impacts of high stress include these:

- impaired memory
- decreased ability to prioritize
- increased rote behavior
- damages to our immune system
- accelerated aging
- weakened ability to think creatively

In addition, high stress is more prevalent among minorities and low socioeconomic groups (Barr, 1997; Carter, 1998; Howard, 2000; Sapolsky, 1998).

Instead of regarding yourself as a teacher, look upon yourself as the person who sets the classroom "state." If the state is warm and secure, the possibility of positive learning occurring is heightened.

Teach anti-stress techniques such as these:

- Begin the day with warm-ups such as *talking circles* (circles where manipulatives are held while talking). This is an opportunity to shed emotional baggage.
- Introduce simple massage practices. This may begin with massaging your own shoulders or those of a friend. (This may not be appropriate in your school, but our teachers found it very effective.)
- Practice breathing techniques, tai chi, or yoga.
- Walk on the grass with bare feet to reduce static electricity.
- Drink filtered water, especially after exercise or computer work.
- Listen to peaceful music.
- Use affirmations that promote a state of calm.
- Allow reluctant readers to read through a finger puppet to lessen perceived stress.

Model behavior:

- Take the time to greet students upon arrival to class.
- Listen, really listen, to them by creating uninterrupted listening time (which may not be right now).
- Begin every day by reviewing the previous day's work through quizzes, mind maps, discussion, summaries, or active reviews. The brain works on patterns and connections rather than isolated incidents. This process provides the opportunity for connection to a theme through a daily or session overview. The ability to make strong, clear connections between learning situations aids understanding and thereby lowers stress.
- Eliminate sarcasm, ridicule, and name-calling. These are all power techniques that stress the brain. Embarrassment can result in the brain/body going through stress similar to a near death experience (Sapolsky, 1998).
- Allow sufficient time and provide resources for a given task.
- Provide overviews. This gives an opportunity for the "global" learners who need the big picture to see how the process works.
- Ensure that the students know what they are expected to learn, how they will be able to learn it, how they will know when they have learned it, and how the new knowledge or skill can be transferred into real life.
- Provide opportunities for movement and manipulative aids such as Koosh® balls[1].
- Allow students to learn through their preferred styles and demonstrate learning through varied intelligences.

One person's stress is another's celebration.

---

1. Koosh® is a registered trademark of ODDZON PRODUCTS, INC.

As a teacher entering a school that had already established effective brain-compatible teaching techniques, I began with something that I personally believed would make a difference with the eleven- to thirteen-year-old students in my class—daily morning shoulder massages. Although considered inappropriate in many schools, our school community was strongly in favor of adopting the practice after the parents and students consented. (The shoulder massages were only conducted in the presence of the teacher.) After some initial reluctance among students, the ritual grew to the point where it became a normal part of the day.

The real evidence that this was a great way to prepare for learning became apparent when outside activities interfered with the students' usual morning massage routine. They would request that the massage session be incorporated later in the day and often used it during DEAR (Drop Everything And Read) sessions that began after lunch.

As the ritual developed, reflection was added, with students telling their partners which massage technique was the best and why. Personal goal setting was also introduced as I, in my role as teacher, provided a quiet overview of the day's expectations.

Massage became a daily expectation for which the students took responsibility. This ensured that they received positive touch as well as reflection time and goal setting in a supportive environment.

An authorized massage can be a very important tool to use in the brain-compatible classroom. It encourages positive and caring touch, is a great state-change, incorporates relaxing or motivating music to assist in setting the tone, and can be used to break down social barriers that can be relevant to certain groups. Imagine how you would feel with a massage to begin each day.

SOURCE: Simon Drewery, former Te Puna teacher and now Principal of Waihi Central School, New Zealand

BRAIN-BASED REVIEW

You put the info in

to take the learning out.

You put reflection in,

and you shake it all about.

You do the "What, so now what?" and you use it soon.

That's what it's all about.

Review and reflection

gives the learning direction.

Review and reflection—

that's what it's all about.

This is the first verse of a review song that I wrote for the "Learn to Learn" program. As with all good learning, review and reflection are vital so let's review your progress.

1. Reminding students what your values are needs to be done regularly. How often do you plan to share "What you will do and what you will never do for them?" Discuss ideas with other adults, and you will gradually expand the number of values that you can share with students. We often don't realize that we have so many. I suggest that you write them down so you can use them again in the future. Maybe you could write them on a chart displayed in the classroom. These could be expanded to include your class's shared values.

2. At this stage of the year, the end of the fifth week and the fifth tool, there would be benefits in reviewing what you have covered so far and also any positive changes that you have noticed in your students' attitudes.

3. Once started, it is important that you continue to use the VIP every week so that it becomes part of the culture. Experiment with different presentation days and styles until you have a working model.

4. "You don't know this about me" could become a journal entry on a daily/weekly basis, growing instead to "I didn't know this about myself." In this way students can see specifically what they learned that day/week and how it changed them.

You keep it practical,

that cures many ills.

You put the music in

and include the movement, too.

You do the self assessment and the peer review.

That's what it's all about.

Review and reflection

gives the learning direction,

Review and reflection—

that's what it's all about.

6

Put-Ups

The mind operates on both the conscious and nonconscious level. The conscious chooses and makes decisions; the nonconscious operates like an auto-pilot (Carter, 2002; Parker, 1993). Raw data are inputted, and if the message is received regularly, the nonconscious mind accepts the idea and tries to bring it into fruition (Murphy, 1997).

The mind is the garden for our thought seeds.

The brain receives its messages either through repetition or through dramatic and highly emotional experiences (Kotulak, 1997). This repetitive message is ingrained through two processes. The first is what we are repeatedly told from external sources, and the second is what we tell ourselves through internal processes. This combination of messages is assimilated and becomes our *self-talk*.

Johansen and Hay (1996) remind us that the nonconscious does not judge. It cannot tell the difference between true and false. Thus, constant or dramatic messages change our internal memories and therefore our self-belief.

After the age of ten, most negative messages are received by internal thought processes rather than external comment (Parker, 1993). This information, this perception, this self-belief, is stored in the auto-pilot. The external result is that we then begin to act out the messages that the nonconscious has accepted (Kehoe, 1999).

We can see this in action when the skilled hypnotist plants a suggestion in the mind of a volunteer. Through suggestion the hypnotist is able to change people's actions and have them behave in another way.

The hypnotist is powerful, but implants the message only once. We have a much greater effect on ourselves because our self-talk is constant. These messages lock us into a pattern of behavior, such as a reaction to a given experience (Murphy, 1997). Often these reactions are emphasized when we are stressed.

What do your internal messages tell you? For example, how do you feel about the following things?

- public speaking
- leading a committee
- your ability to make decisions
- your coordination
- your attractiveness to others

All of these views have been formed as a result of how we perceive experiences, what others have lead us to believe, and what we have told ourselves through self-talk (Politano & Paquin, 2000; Robbins, 1991). This is why the words that we use with ourselves and with others are so important and why modeling self-belief completes the picture. "Put-ups," the opposite of put-downs, can help your learners reinforce their positive self-beliefs and discount the self-beliefs that are negative.

Ensure an emotionally safe environment by taking these steps:

- Constantly and vigilantly operate a "put-up zone" in the school where only positive comments to both yourself and others are allowed. Model this as a staff and in relationships with each other.
- Practice compliments sessions with students of all ages. Model these with compliments in the staff room.
- Eliminate sarcasm.
- Share metaphors and real-life stories of success.
- Bring in role models and life coaches who can reinforce the positive message.
- Teach students that hormones can have a major effect on moods, but that relaxation, affirmations, and exercise techniques will help minimize their effect.
- Explain to students that put-ups are acknowledged with two words: "Thank you."

You create your own personal reality in your mind.

7

Breathing Techniques

Breathing is one of the essentials of life, but it is often neglected as an aid for learning.

Because the brain's main role is survival, it is easily affected by anything that appears to be dangerous. This "danger" can be constantly present in the learning environment for many students. It is impossible for the teacher to eliminate all stress as it is based on learner's perceptions, not always reality. Also, the removal of all stress would not be beneficial, as without some, we would not get up in the morning.

If we view something as stressful, our bodies react with the production of stress hormones (Sapolsky, 1998). It is reduction of and coping with high-level stress that is important. There is a long-term benefit, therefore, in teaching stress-reduction techniques to learners (Cameron-Hill & Yates, 2000; Glazener, 2004).

Controlled breathing is an effective stress-reduction technique. It slows the metabolism and gives the brain an opportunity to move blood from the stress centers to areas of higher-level thinking where decisions can be made (Gelb, 1995; Joseph, 2002; Sapolsky, 1998; Wilson, 1995).

BREATHING TO PROMOTE A STATE OF CALM

- Stand tall in a relaxed state with one hand on the chest and the other just below the navel.
- Breathe in through the nose and exhale nosily through the mouth.
- Repeat five to ten times, concentrating only on the feeling of air entering and leaving your body.
- As you become more advanced in the technique, try to breathe using your stomach rather than your chest. This is called "belly-" or "baby-breathing."

Young babies do it, and it reduces the pressure on internal organs. If you are doing it correctly, the hand on your chest will not rise, but the one below your navel will.

- Combining this with movement such as tai chi is highly effective. All of these exercises can be combined with visualization techniques.
- I find that these are great exercises to use when students arrive back in class from a break, daily fitness, or working in another area of the school. I greet them at the door and speak to them in a very quiet voice asking them to form a circle within the classroom space. Then we enter the breathing routine as a group. The voice remains quiet to maximize the state-change as the students move to their leaning centers.
- Controlled breathing also works well if students are falling behind in their work during a test or if they are having difficulty remembering a question or answer.

BREATHING TO PROMOTE ANGER MANAGEMENT

- Complete the calm breathing as above, but count to ten, three times between breaths. It really works!
- Breathe through a tightened mouth and then relax the mouth for the exhale. Liken this to zipping and unzipping the lips. This will be a different style of breathing and will need concentration. This change of focus works by lessening the concentration on the anger.
- Walk and breathe rapidly and then deliberately; slowing the body down can be advantageous.
- Tear up paper with rapid breaths, roll the paper into a ball with slower breathing, and finally hold your breath as you calm and throw the paper at a target.

BREATHING TO ENHANCE ENERGY

In the middle of an afternoon, this is very handy. Use the same technique of breathing through the abdomen, but this time, use it to energize.

- Breathe in to a count of four.
- Hold for a count of sixteen.
- Release fully for a count of eight.
- *This works by eliminating more carbon dioxide from the respiratory system.*
- Repeat ten times to lift energy during those cyclic down times.
- Add a glass of water for increased effect.

Perhaps something we need to remember in the Western world is the power of the human breath.

8

Relaxation

Very little positive learning happens when students are in a poor learning state (Howard, 2000). In fact, learning is so state-dependent that the reading and creating of optimal learning conditions may be one of the most crucial roles that a teacher plays.

As teachers, we have all had those times when the lesson flows. Student answers lead automatically into the next important point. Learners are enthusiastic, the atmosphere is very positive—this is "flow." Stress is low, and the learner is reluctant to end the session.

This state cannot be created through sheer willpower but can be altered through relaxation techniques (Allica, 1990; Cameron-Hill & Yates, 2000; Glazener, 2004).

Relaxation can be achieved through a variety of ways, but these are the most effective:

- breathing
- postural changes
- affirmations
- listening to music or relaxing to sounds such as chiming bells
- listening to positive relaxation tapes

One of the easiest ways to alter our state is to change body posture. Sitting up, chin up and eyes wide open, especially accompanied by a smile, will promote a positive attitude. Tensing and then relaxing various muscle groups while standing, lying on the floor, or sitting cross-legged with a straight back will help develop awareness of body tension (Allica, 1990).

n.b. Lying down and/or closing eyes in public can be stressful for many people and needs slow and careful introduction. For some students this will take up to six months and should never be insisted upon.

Stress builds up hormones in our body creating the flight or fight syndrome. The quickest way to remove these hormones is to increase blood flow through exercising (Sapolsky, 1998). This is why walking is beneficial when we are angry. Many teachers at our school allow students to walk outside within view of the classroom when they need a state-change. However, before we return to the learning state, we need to slow down. Controlled breathing, tai chi, or massage will all help.

Choice over the learning position can reduce stress. Classrooms should include space for lying or stretching out, cushions for relaxed sitting, lecterns for those who enjoy standing and working or think best with their feet ground, and rocking chairs for soothing repetitive movements for those with limited crawl development or high stress levels. Arrange free areas where kinesthetic learners can walk inside and, if applicable, outside the classroom. Allow students to position their chairs so that their back is to the wall or so they are facing the door. This allows them to have a clear view if someone is approaching.

Touch stimulates positive hormones and reduces stress. Young babies soon recognize the value of good touching (Silberg, 1999). Indeed, research confirms that babies who are cuddled and massaged advance more quickly in both social and academic areas (Diamond & Hopson, 1998). Massage stimulates the nerve endings and is known to promote new cell growth in stroke victims. We introduced massage at our school for these reasons, however you may decide that it is not appropriate for a variety of reasons. When massaging, have students work with a partner rather than sitting in a circle. This is because we cannot give and receive at the same time. Because of safety issues, limit massage to the shoulder and neck area and accompany with soft music.

There are many pleasant and peaceful music selections that promote health and calm. Generally they are best without lyrics. "When you're looking for comfort, music with the heartbeat effect can be like a return to the womb" (Miles, 1997, p. 63). This effect has a beat at between sixty to eighty beats per minute. Some baroque music is ideal for this effect; however, listen to it first as there is a range in this genre, and some will sound more appealing than others. New age music and favorites such as Burt Bacharach's "Raindrops Keep Falling on My Head" or "My Favorite Things" from *The Sound of Music* are also worthwhile (Campbell, 1992). Keep the volume at a minimum and explain to learners the differing learning benefits of a wide range of music.

It is the relaxed mind that discovers the genius within.

9

Eliminating Extrinsic Rewards

Our discussion regarding rewards sparked a lot of debate at our school. Like most schools, we had used rewards for a long time. However, the changes that we introduced produced positive results and had us thinking much more about the deeper issues involved. Our changed approach meant that incentives were still able to be given, however the timing and the purpose behind the giving changed.

The human brain operates differently in a rewards-based environment. Extrinsic rewards increase stress because the brain now operates in an anxious and competitive state, focusing is on the prize rather than the learning. This in turn inhibits creativity, cooperative learning, problem solving, and recall (Kohn, 1996). Extrinsic rewards are manipulative. They are used as a control mechanism (Glasser, 1992, 1993). Research indicates that people who operate a reward system will also favor the use of punishment (Kohn, 1996).

What are the characteristics of extrinsic rewards?

- They are given by another person or institution.
- They have a "market value" in the social setting in which they are given.
- To be effective, they must be known about in advance.
- They operate on exclusion and are therefore unfair.
- They are usually given to reward a result that is easy to assess. Process and effort are often not rewarded as these are more difficult to monitor.
- They can only be granted for a predicted result, but many creative and gifted ideas—our moments of genius that we all experience—occur

unexpectedly. They cannot be predicted and therefore cannot be rewarded.

- Their benefits are short-lived, and the degree of reward always needs to be increased.

SOURCE: Kohn, 1993.

Students who have records of poor behavior are even less likely to respond with any significance to rewards. This is because the area in the brain for perceptual mapping and self-discipline, the prefrontal cortex, is less likely to be engaged if the perception is that control is held by another. This may explain why low achievers and nonengaged learners appear to be unmotivated. The more they perceive control, the more they will adopt negative behavior. It is not logical but is an emotional response to threat.

Extrinsic rewards

- reduce satisfaction, which is intrinsic motivation.
- lessen the understanding that the best things in life come as a result of anticipation, striving for improvement as a result of making mistakes, and the effort needed to accomplish the goal.
- reduce the person's ability to be a successful and satisfied human.

If certificates, trophies, or stickers are given as part of a predictable arrangement, they are rewards. Instead, you can replace them with celebration and acknowledgement. A positive comment can be given to acknowledge progress or certificates and stickers can be given in an unpredictable manner as a celebration of achievement (Kohn, 1993).

The goal should not be the trophy, but rather the intrinsic satisfaction of achievement.

However, be aware that once an acknowledgement or celebration is given, it is easy for the learner to expect it again if they repeat the behavior. If they are given out too regularly, they will become the "carrot" and as such, they are now a reward. This needs constant awareness and monitoring by the teacher.

Satisfaction is deeply rewarding.

Stickers, prizes, or others forms of rewards were the most obvious targets for our school's anti-extrinsic rewards campaign. However, we also noticed that other rewards were offered, often unconsciously. We had a newly arrived staff member who was learning the brain-compatible philosophy that had by then been operating in the school for five years. As I was talking to this teacher in her room one day, I noticed a chart on the wall. It was titled "Home Learning." The chart had all of the students' names down one side and a grid for the ten weeks of the term. After the fifth week was a specially colored column. This column related to the first four weeks of home learning and the statement read, "If you have completed your home learning, and it has consistently achieved the criteria stated below, then you can have week five free."

We read the statement together, and I asked the teacher, "If we let prisoners out of jail early through the parole system, what are we saying?"

"That prison is not a nice place to be," the teacher replied.

"If we let students out of school early as a reward for a good day's work, what are we really saying?"

"That school is like a jail and a good place to leave."

"What does this chart actually say about home learning?"

The teacher immediately saw the connection and the next day proudly showed me the new chart. At week five it now stated; "Because home learning is so important, if you complete the first four weeks and achieve the criteria stated below, in week five, you may choose from the home learning list attached."

A subtle but very important message about learning.

10

Punishment and Consequences

Punishment in this section is defined as *a purely spontaneous emotional reaction rather than a logical response to an incident.* The problem with punishments is that because they are given in haste and are often excessive, they are frequently reneged upon and even apologized for (Biddulph & Biddulph, 1998). The student then learns that he only need to wait or plead innocence and then the punishment is reduced or removed altogether. If the excessive punishments are not reduced, they are perceived as unfair and a rift develops between student and teacher (Faber & Mazlish, 1996). "You will never go on another class trip while I am your teacher" is a statement that is easy to give and difficult to remove. It is a no-win situation.

Stress hormones create our emotional reaction. As you are now aware, the reaction to these hormones inhibits the decision-making area of the brain and reduces logical response and common sense (Joseph, 2002; Sapolsky, 1998).

At our school, we defined a consequence as something that is discussed when the mood of all parties has returned to a state of calm. Its purpose is emotional coaching so that life skills are enhanced (Gordon, 1997; Gottman & Declaire, 1997). Students discuss probable consequences of actions in advance as part of life skills education. During this process, choices are examined and possible negative or positive consequences are examined. The student can then make choices with a wider knowledge of what is likely to happen. This is an essential life skill and assists with the development of both common sense and empathy (Gordon, 1997).

Punishments focus on the negative and are viewed as a "quick fix." Consequences focus on learning to make positive choices and are a longer-term process.

PUNISHING STATEMENTS: HOW TO AVOID THEM

Punishment may be the first thing that comes to mind in a difficult situation. It is important to take time to make a more informed judgment that has positive and effective results. This is a learned skill and requires continual practice. Try these techniques:

- Remove either the student or yourself from the situation. Time-out has great benefits. A buddy teacher may be a good person to help here.
- Practice your own anti-stress techniques by moving, breathing, and counting to ten. You may need to do this more than once.
- During the time-out, develop a clear process of thinking strategies that the student can follow once he has achieved a state of calm. These may include statements about how he has affected himself by his actions, what he will do next, and setting goals for the future.
- Allow time for both parties to calm down and then discuss the situation without the negative emotions.
- Remember that when your response is purely emotional, the other party is *pulling your strings* and the only way to regain control of yourself is to cut them (see Tool 28).
- Rather than asking why, ask questions beginning with "what." These are more factual and easier to answer.
- Use "I" statements about how you were affected. However, avoid the "I want you to" statements since these are controlling and do not promote growth. Instead, explore possibilities of what the student is going to do to rectify the situation. This may require coaching.
- Have clear consequences for the student's action that are seen as fair because a clear "why" is provided. "The reason that we cannot have this behavior is because . . . and therefore . . . ."
- If an apology is involved, it must be sincere and not coerced—otherwise it is a waste of time.
- Clearly share the framework of this process with the class on a regular basis. This could become part of the Rules, Guidelines, and Agreements process (see Tool 3).
- Develop a multi-faceted life-skills program that teaches self-discipline and social skills on a schoolwide basis (see Part III: Promoting Understanding).

If we don't punish a learner who cannot read, why do we punish them when they lack social skills?

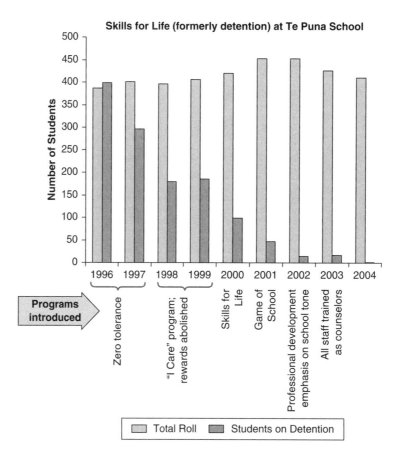

BEHAVIORAL CHANGES

In 1996 the school roll was 387 students ranging in age from five to thirteen years. If students misbehaved during recess or the lunch break, a duty teacher could put them on detention. The strategy was reactive. This happened on 399 occasions during that year! Some students came back onto the program up to thirty times. Apart from coping, there was no real schoolwide plan to deal with the situation. Something was not working properly. We had just begun to introduce a brain-compatible philosophy, but it was still undergoing heavy refinement and development.

In the beginning, the detention process entailed a loss of students' leisure time during which I supervised them as they wrote out lines such as "I must not swear at other students." We operated a zero-tolerance for misbehavior during the first few years. In fact, in 1997 there were 100 fewer students in the detention program, but it was not until 1998 that a noticeable and positive change occurred.

First Major Refinement

During that year, we introduced the concept of the "I Care" program with these four statements: "I care for myself, I care for others, I care for property, and I care for the environment." These statements virtually replaced all rules and became a central core from which to plan out teaching and behavioral programs. Instead of writing lines like "I must not swear at other students," students now wrote out one statement and filled in the details.

"I care for myself and I care for others because people are important. I care for property and I care for the environment because this is my world.

I didn't care for . . . when I . . . . Because I am a caring person, next time I will . . . ."

During the process, I would continually discuss the student's choices. Asking how others felt was too difficult a concept for young students to grasp. Instead, I always revolved the conversation around the question, "How have you cared for yourself?" When students began to see that their decisions resulted in positive or negative consequences for themselves, then change began to happen.

By this time, enrollment had climbed, but detentions had dropped from 399 to 180.

Second Major Refinement

By 1999 the "I care" statements were the official school philosophy. Stress reduction techniques were practiced in most classrooms, and the results were very positive. We had observed how tired students were, especially during the hot summer months, so we changed our timetable into three ninety-minute blocks, with a recess break of thirty minutes in the morning; the lunch break was shortened from sixty to fifty minutes.

The "Skills for Life" program had more depth and moved away from punishment. Instead, we focused on students' learning about themselves and their behaviors and the skills they would need in life. The additions looked more at why we behave and react the way that we do. As part of this program, senior students were introduced to a small program called "The Twenty Rules of the Game of School and How to Play It." I designed a small booklet that summarized these rules, and it was mailed to the students after their first term at high school to remind them of our continual relationship with them.

Rather than punishing to achieve results, the emphasis was placed on up-skilling students and empowering them with the ability to make better choices. Detention was officially renamed "Skills for Life," and I always began by communicating with students that the time would be spent on improving their opportunities and skills to make more informed choices. These conversations were centered on the analogy that "life is a game, and, to win the game, you need to know the rules. Unfortunately, these rules are unwritten, but this time will be spent in exploring those that are appropriate."

When speaking with boys, I used the term "winning choices," as in my experience they tend to be very competitive and often reject rules. When speaking with girls, I often related their behavior to "being good," as we found that they were more often motivated to conform.

I used a lot of props, including visuals markers such as Koosh® balls, which could be placed on the floor to provide a visual/spatial representation of where people were in relationships or in that particular situation. This helped to make an abstract concept more concrete, especially in spatial relationship terms. Puppets (see Part III, Tool 27 for details), flowcharts, and Venn diagrams worked well to show how choices lead to consequences. Role-plays to explore what happened and metaphors about life choices were also effective (see Tool 2).

During the discussions, we explored multiple options. It was important for students to understand clearly that they had made the choices. Choices were neither good nor bad, however all choices lead to consequences and they needed to be aware of this.

During this same period, the use of external rewards was dramatically reduced.

Our brain-compatible philosophy was growing, and our teachers were more confident in using a range of tools in the classroom. The schoolwide "Learn to Learn" program was introduced (see Part III), and the emphasis moved from pure teaching to helping the students understand how they learned.

Previously we had spent time studying the concepts of learning styles and multiple intelligences. Now we wanted students to use that knowledge so they could work towards a degree of personal mastery. Students were more involved in their learning, and a degree of choice became a part of all curriculum areas. All classes introduced clear learning intentions into the curriculum, and these were shared with students. In addition, assessment practices moved away from summative to formative, with students involved to a high degree. All students were encouraged to attend staff-parent interviews; from Grade 6, students ran this process.

These changes worked especially well for our indigenous Maori students who were in our Maori language immersion classes and also for students who had previously been considered at-risk regarding their learning and behavior. The new style of learning involving movement and choice suited their learning needs. The detention rate for our Maori immersion students, which had been very high, plummeted to zero and stayed there for the next five years.

"Skills for Life" was comprehensive and reduced detention numbers to a low of fourteen, while school enrollment was more than 450 students.

Third Major Refinement

The third refinement was all about people. Why did we react the way that we did? Why do people bring certain behaviors to certain situations? In 2003, all of our staff was involved in an intensive counseling course. We used William Glasser's (1989) concept of "reality therapy" as the basis for the course and added brain research regarding reaction to stress, states, and emotions to support it.

Reality therapy (see Tool 25) is a very simple yet effective strategy that we used in combination with an anti-bullying program, a curriculum involving movement, hands-on activities, and a philosophy based on people rather than curriculum. As a result, only one student was involved in the "Skills for Life" program (formerly detention) in 2003, and he was put on detention by the caretaker/janitor who hadn't been part of the counseling course.

Learning and behavior is the same thing.

BRAIN-BASED REVIEW

First of all, you will probably not have had instant and successful change in all areas. Change can be very messy, and you may be tempted to give up, especially if you encounter problems—which of course you will. Problems allow us to grow and stretch our abilities. Unfortunately, some people only see the problem and rather than growing new skills by moving through it, they use the opportunity to reinforce poor self-esteem by giving up.

Deep change takes time. Decide on the tools that you wish to develop further and make a plan. Share it with a trusted colleague so that she can help you believe in what you are doing.

I have listed some starter questions below and left a space for you to write questions that you will wish to ask of yourself. You will find that certain types of questions are more beneficial. "What" and "how" questions give us something to build upon positively. "Why" questions lead us down dead end roads. "Why does this always happen to me?" Back comes the instant self-talk reply, "Because I'm stupid, careless, etc." Not very beneficial for personal growth, but great for personal put-downs.

Questions help the reticular activating system to focus. Allow time, and the answers will come:

1. What time of day have you found best to practice anti-stress techniques?

2. What modifications have you found successful to suit your particular work environment?

3. If you have modified any of the tools, are you still retaining their essential purpose?

4. Are you using any new teaching techniques related to any of the first ten tools? Please e-mail me at scaddan.mike@gmail.com and let me know of your successes.

5. Do you have certain times in the day when you use planned emotional bonding techniques? These may vary from class to class.

6. Do you notice any significant patterns of behavior and learning developing? If so, how can you continue to develop these positively?

7. Eliminating extrinsic rewards can be a long process. How is your plan developing? Keep going on it. It's worth the journey.

8. What questions are you planning to ask yourself so that the development continues?

PART II

Developing Patterns and Coherence

11

Contamination

The brain contaminates very easily. We all have places in which we do not feel comfortable because of previous experiences. We see this when observing a patient sitting in the dentist's waiting room. The individual may appear calm, but as soon as the sound of the drill is heard, anxiety rises as the association is made to a past experience.

This can also happen at school. If the same area of the classroom is used for learning and for disciplining, after time the brain will confuse the two (DePorter, Reardon, & Singer-Nourie, 1999). The classroom area becomes contaminated in the same way as the dentist's waiting room. Stress levels rise, the subconscious fear response takes over, and students may misbehave so that they are removed from that environment.

Because being alone is also stressful for most students, the next time a similar situation occurs, they often involve a friend. Now, even though a punishment may occur, they can support each other, which is generally less stressful.

This is a normal stress response known as "flight." The same response can happen when the student feels unable to complete a task and therefore feels inadequate. It is easier to ignore the work at hand rather than to confront your fears and deal with them. This may be part of learned helplessness (Howard, 2000). This condition will continue as long as the student links that particular area or subject with failure. If we want students to change their responses (Dispenza, 2007), we need to change some of the conditions that create the undesirable behavior.

WHAT TO DO

As the teacher, learn to manage the classroom state rather than managing students:

- Allow for a certain degree of choice in seating and production of work.
- Consider having specific areas for instruction, for discipline, for great learning tips, and for metaphors/stories. This will help the learner to

associate **learning** through conditioned response (DePorter, Reardon, & Singer-Nourie, 1999; Sprenger, 2003).

- I used to include a "guaranteed success area" in the classroom where learners could go to achieve. I would work with them to help them see even the smallest improvement. This became a popular location for many students to visit each day and learn to believe in themselves. The next step was to transfer this belief to other areas by having them visit the "success area" in their minds.
- Disciplining should be done in private whenever possible, away from peers and the learning environment.
- Teach students to be aware of their own stress signs and motivators so they learn to take early corrective action. These motivators are dealt with in Part III of this book.
- Have safe areas where students can practice their own stress release practices. This area then becomes associated with positive solutions. We developed and taught students the following strategies for reducing stress:
  - Tear paper to help reduce stress hormones.
  - Use calm breathing techniques.
  - Walk in a very large pair of shoes. It is difficult to do, creates a new problem for the brain to solve, and is humorous.
  - Walk a circuit while focusing on breathing.
  - Write a letter of frustration—read it, amend it, and share it with a trusted adult.
  - Draw the situation.
  - Avoid asking yourself why you did something and instead concentrate on what you wanted and what you learned from it (see Tool 26).
  - Visualize the "puppet strings" and cutting them (see Tool 27).

As the students become more proficient at self-management, they can remain in class but imagine/visualize themselves in the safe area and achieve the same results.

Following these procedures will help students to control themselves and replace negative responses with positive ones. This helps develop a pattern of coherent learning.

Be aware that many parents have a contaminated view of school or learning that is entrenched as a result of circumstances. This may result in them sharing comments with their children such as "I was never good at spelling either" or "You should be much better at art since everyone in our family is good at drawing." Constant dialogue with parents is needed to make them more aware of this tendency.

Education is not about punishment or control. It is about helping the person to move forward in his or her personal journey.

This section began with a tool regarding contamination. I have become more aware that contamination can occur in many forms. Sometimes we are enjoying a magic moment with the class or student, an introduction, review, story, or pertinent point when . . . . there is a knock on the door and a monitor brings in a message.

Feedback from local teachers is that they are being constantly interrupted during prime teaching times. If this is happening in your institution, perhaps it is time to discuss ways to lessen the negative effect. In this age of instant gratification, we are used to expecting instant replies. However your prime purpose is to assist learners to develop as people. Possibly the message senders are unaware of the constant flow of interruptions that you may be experiencing.

While some messages are important, I'm sure that others can wait. Perhaps there can be established message times during the day and we can plan around them. I'm sure that there are others ways of dealing with this issue. A number of schools that I work with have developed plans that designate only certain times during the school day when interruptions may take place. I am watching how this develops; even though there may be some growing pains, it sounds like a great idea to begin with.

12

Cycles of Concentration

Our brain is affected by many cycles during the learning day (Jensen, 2006). A cycle is a change in hormonal levels resulting in varying degrees of energy, concentration, memory, hunger, thirst, strength, and enthusiasm (Brewer & Campbell, 1991).

Two of these are the low-to-high energy cycle and the relaxation-to-tension cycle. Because these cycles affect both our positive feelings and our energy levels, they have a major influence on our learning and our perception (Brewer & Campbell, 1991; Smith, 2004). It is essential that learners become aware of their own cycles.

ENERGY CYCLES

- As adults and pre-adolescents, we normally move to full energy between thirty and sixty minutes after getting up in the morning (Schacter, 1996).
- Energy rhythms follow cycles of 90 to 110 minutes. During this time we experience a full range of feelings from high to low energy and low to high (Brewer & Campbell, 1991).
- Some cycles can be very obvious with sudden plunges and corresponding highs of energy.
- For most of us there is an energy plunge in the afternoon.
- Most learners can focus better in the late morning and early afternoon time slots; between 9 a.m. and 2 p.m. is optimal. Be aware that teenagers operate on a later cycle-pattern and function better into the afternoon and evening (Schacter, 1996).

- These circadian rhythms are affected by sunlight, so we tend to be more optimistic on bright days or during summer and more pessimistic on dull days or during winter (Howard, 2000).
- Because our body clock is related to the sun, events such as sleep-ins on weekends and holidays, as well adjusting the clock for daylight savings, can have a major effect on many people. It is estimated that the time change due to daylight savings affects our energy cycles for up to three weeks (Howard, 2000).

MEMORY CYCLES

- Because 9 to 11 a.m. is better for short-term memory for most people, this is a great time for spelling, problem solving, math, science, and writing (Brewer & Campbell, 1991).
- Noon to 2 p.m. appears to be better for movement, computing, music, singing, and art (Brewer & Campbell, 1991).
- The period from 2 to 5 p.m. is better for literature, social studies, sports, and drama (Brewer & Campbell, 1991).
- Generally it is better to teach new material in the morning and subjects that are more people- and experience-related in the afternoon (Brewer & Campbell, 1991).
- Although the timing of individual cycles is unique, they consistently follow 90- to 120-minute patterns, so it makes sense to schedule subjects into these time frames. This means that all learners will complete a cycle in their own individual way during this time frame (Howard, 2000).
- In addition, it is better to divide these time frames into twenty-minute slots during which something is introduced, practiced, and reviewed. This fits in well with what is understood about primacy (memory is stronger at the beginning of a session) and recency (the second strongest memory time is at the end of a session). Time frames of twenty minutes rather than forty-five or ninety minutes means that there is less downtime in the middle practice session where memory potential is lessened (Baddeley, 2004).
- Because learners are operating at different parts of their concentration cycles, move the timing of tests and reviews on a weekly basis so that all learners have the opportunity to work through a concentration peak period (Howard, 2000).
- Hemispheric cycles are also 90 to 120 minutes. During these times we will operate better sequentially (slightly more left-brain focused) or globally (slightly more right-brain focused). Regular state-changers using music, movement, and water intake will help to balance these cycles (Howard, 2000).

It is not what they cover but what they learn that is important.

13

State-Changes

The brain is not designed to maintain attention. Its primary role is survival, so it needs to be constantly scanning incoming information (Jensen, 2005).

Any input that is not stimulating or relevant will be largely ignored and rapidly deleted.

A guideline for attention in the classroom is to convert the learner's age into minutes—a five-year-old can concentrate for approximately five minutes and then he needs a change of state to maintain attention (Allen, 2002).

To maintain this attention, the teacher needs to provide state-changes when she observes that the learner is slipping away over the "crest of the wave" (Allen, 2002, p. 28). Signs of this include fidgeting, yawning, requests to go to the toilet, and increased noise levels and off-task behaviors.

Rather than being a manager of the curriculum, the effective teacher needs to understand how to manage states. A state-change ensures that the entire group is actively involved in an experience together (Robbins, 1996).

State-changes work best if they involve these activities:

- movement
- thinking
- movement
- predicting
- movement
- summarizing
- movement
- discussion
- movement

Did you pick up that all state-changes require movement? These changes are important when you are starting the day and after breaks as they help to focus the learner.

Learners use their own state-changers such as talking, going to the toilet, or looking out of the window. These, as already discussed, are important signs for the teacher to be aware of and monitor.

State-changers are best when combined with the learning that is currently happening. At this stage a clear relationship can be established so that learners becomes more aware of themselves and the need for a state-change.

A simple state-change technique may run as follows:

- Please stand.
- Move two steps and find a partner.
- Think about what we have just covered in the topic.
- Rate it as a *1*, *2*, or *3* with *3* being that you strongly agree, *2* that you are uncertain, and *1* that you strongly disagree.
- Compare your ratings with your partner's and discuss why you rated it the way you did.

A state-change may be an energy booster such as a "stand up and stretch" activity. It could be a mini-break with a task to move to upon return. It may involve mind mapping, a group activity, or a discussion. There are hundreds of options.

The important thing for the teacher is to sense the "crest of the wave." Once learners move past this point, it is difficult to bring them back (Allen, 2002).

Sometimes we push on because of time constraints and curriculum coverage.
It is not worth it. Slow down and make learning a journey.

I often have the students stand up and tell three or four different people what they have learned, enjoyed, or want to know more about in the lesson so far. This adds more substance to the lesson and tends to refocus the students while staying in tune with what is being learned. When they return to their desks or groups, they are always a lot more attentive and ask and answer more productive and effective questions.

SOURCE: Shannon Robinson, elementary teacher in New Zealand and England

14

Crossovers

For more than fifty years, pioneers in behavioral optometry and sensory-motor training have been studying the effects of movement (Calvin, 1996). We now understand that if we restrict movement, we restrict sensory processing of incoming information. This is because movement, especially of the head, changes the focus of the eyes, which in turn activates the brain to increase input processing (Hannaford, 1995). It is a survival mechanism that we can use to good effect in the classroom.

You will have noticed that people nod and move their body during a conversation. This is not just a social convention to reassure our partner that we are listening. We also do it when we are talking on the telephone. Rather, it is done to assist us in processing information. Movement even changes our way of speaking, including the tone, and perceiving meaning (Robbins, 1996).

We now know that learning is a complex interchange between the mind and the body. Movement helps us access many parts of the brain, allowing complex processing to occur. When the movement consistently crosses the midline—the invisible line that could be drawn from our forehead down our nose, sternum, and beyond to finish between our feet—it has a heightened effect (Hannaford, 1993).

HOW AND WHY DOES THIS HAPPEN?

Brains are unique and as a result of the effects of genes, stress drugs, toxins, and nurturing, all function at differing levels. This can result in the brain developing non-integrated and lopsided functioning processes. Movement across the midline can help to alleviate this by creating new neural pathways (Hannaford, 1995).

We also know that the hippocampus continues to produce new brain cells throughout your entire life and that these migrate to specific areas. Because the brain works on a "use it or lose it" principle, areas that are activated frequently grow, while little used areas do not (Hannaford, 1995). This is why crossover exercises are effective.

Because the brain is "plastic" in its ability to change, these exercises stimulate the corpus collosum, the part of the brain that joins both hemispheres. This stimulation kick-starts development in areas where activity was minimal, allowing the brain to constantly reorganize.

These exercises are based on three simple premises:

- Learning is a natural and joyous activity.
- Learning blocks create an inability to overcome stress and cope with new or difficult tasks.
- Because there is less movement in modern life, we all have these learning blocks.

Crossovers involve touch and movement, both of which are beneficial. If we use stimulating movement and positive emotions such as humor, we enhance the effect. It is impossible to separate emotion from learning and thinking. Emotions are the gateway, and brain crossover exercises can be one of many keys. Stress restricts learning. Movement eases stress; therefore, movement increases the possibility of cognitive performance (Hannaford, 1995).

Here are some guidelines for using the exercises:

- The midline that needs to be crossed is the area where the left and right focal fields overlap requiring the eyes and their respective muscles to work as a team so that the two eyes can function as one (Hannaford, 1995).
- The midline runs down through the center of our body. Both our body and head need to be kept straight as you do these exercises as well as during handwriting and reading to promote effective hand-eye coordination (Cohen & Goldsmith, 2002).
- Begin with large movements and graduate to small ones.
- Read specific exercise literature to find out which exercises will best stimulate which processes.
- Use these before the learning session and as a state-change.
- Explain to learners why and how they work.
- Everyone can benefit from consistent exercises.

All learning is a mind-and-body experience.

I use crossover exercises a lot in my classroom. Once I have taught the movement and I have explained the benefit to the students, we practice and then use the exercises in the appropriate situations. Before written sessions is a favorite time.

During a writing session one day, I was about to reprimand a little girl who consistently produced the bare minimum amount of work. She got out of her chair yet again, but this time I refrained from intervening. I'm so glad! I watched her as she went to a quiet corner of the classroom and began the crossover exercises that she had learned for creative writing. She began with the large movements that we had practiced and then moved progressively to the smaller. After a few minutes she returned to her seat and produced more written work than I had ever seen her do. This was student power in action.

SOURCE: Shannon Robinson, elementary teacher in New Zealand and England

BRAIN-BASED REVIEW

In regard to Tools 11–14, consider these questions:

1. Are you more aware of concentration cycles, both yours and the students'?

2. How is your awareness of these cycles reflected in either the timetable or the way you teach?

3. Are there positive improvements that you could share with other staff?

4. Do you notice positive changes regarding discipline as a result of using any of the stress-reducing techniques suggested? Some of these may be subtle.

5. Do you have any suggestions to add? If so, write them down and share them with others. It is important that we add to the positive development of our profession.

6. What are the favorite state-changes in your class?

Remember to continue some state-changes so that they become a ritual. Sometimes I introduced new reviews and state-changes when the students wanted to continue with what was known. It's a fine line.

Our staff found that putting crossovers to music worked well. Simple tunes with a constant beat and repetitive verses were especially suitable. The "Monster Mash" by Bobby "Boris" Pickett, "Purple People Eater" by Sheb Wooley, "I'd Like to Teach the World to Sing" by the New Seekers, and "In the Summer Time When the Weather Is Fine" by Mungo Jerry all provide a steady beat for the exercises.

15

Improving Memory Links

Research suggests that more than ninety-eight percent of learning is non-conscious (Gazzaniga, 2001; Jensen, 2005; Sousa, 2005). As educators we need to make certain that the important information we want to be retained is delivered through the two percent of processing channels that are conscious. We know memory is fickle; how can we as teachers ensure that important information is retained?

There are five memory pathways that we use: semantic (often referred to as content without context), episodic (memory of events related to time and order), conditioned response (memory enhanced through repetition and response), procedural (involving memory of skills such as riding a bike), and emotional (strong personal experiences). The emotional pathway is the strongest while semantic is the weakest because it often has no clear context (Dispenza, 2007; Sprenger, 2003).

We also believe that younger learners take in information best through smell (olfactory), tactile, kinesthetic, and visual input and learn least through the auditory (listening) process. Therefore, it makes sense to create memory through a combination of movement, emotion, visual aids, and hands-on experiences (Prashnig, 1998; Sprenger, 2003). Here are some suggestions for doing this:

- Use the whiteboard, mind maps, or charts to give a strong, colorful visual overview, main points, and a summary.
- List main points as they are completed using key words.
- Use a prop such as an arrow to show what is going to be targeted or the main points of the next session.
- Wear a bright hat to emphasize important information.
- Hold up or wear a flashing light to review the essential elements of the session.

- Use humor or emotional stories such as metaphors to strengthen memory.
- Create memory mood with dramatic music.
- Move and discuss the main ideas. Movement produces norepinephrine, a neurotransmitter that acts as "memory glue."
- Have students stand to receive important information.
- Clap while they chant the important points.
- Have students make up advertisements, songs, or poems that "sell" their learning.
- Use the lyrics of well-known songs to accentuate the message.
- Write songs about the topic using well-known tunes.
- Stand on a chair to deliver point of view.
- Wear a period costume.
- Repeat the main points as a pledge in an emotional voice.
- Have students write a short note about their learning. Mail the notes back to them at a later date.
- Use taste and aromas to create mood.
- Use a train whistle, chimes, or buzzer to introduce an important point.
- Allow students to present information through art, drama, technology, or traditional methods.
- Allow time for learners to discuss, question, predict, and of course, to teach others.
- Use field trips and real-life experiences to cement memory.
- Allow time to practice skills. Practicing makes skills permanent—so make sure that students are doing it correctly!
- Allow time for students to review their learning on a regular basis.

It's not what we know, but what we know we know that is important.

Learners love to know what they know!

My students love review games, and if I am pushed for time or forget them, they beg that we do them.

After every new topic session, we do a review game of some sort. I had noticed that students loved sharing new things that they had learned in this fun and, at times, noisy manner. We always review the last session in a sequence before moving on to the next section and then review again at the end using questions generated by the students themselves. Even though they were only aged seven to nine years, they became very capable of asking sophisticated questions and providing in-depth answers.

SOURCE: Shannon Robinson, elementary teacher in New Zealand and England

If you need more memory-enhancing techniques, try these:

- If you are asking students to record on a mind map or even in conventional notes, let them know how many main points you are covering to assist them with spacing.

- Use key musical tracks to prewire the main points. *Adrenaline to Go* by the Brain Store (2002) has some great tracks for this.
- Prepare questions on the topic where the answer relates to letters of the alphabet. Each team takes turns to choose a letter and see if they can answer the question. For example, if a team chose the letter *L* in a geography lesson, the question might be, "What is the capital of England." Remember to save your alphabet clues for following years.
- Have students write important points in color, capital letters, or with the nondominant hand.
- Repeat material to a partner.
- Toss Koosh® balls or Frisbees®[1] around while playing music. When the music stops, those people holding the Koosh® ball/Frisbee® state a key point from the topic. To reduce stress, allow them to ask a partner on either side to assist if required.
- Use mind maps, flowcharts, or graphic organizers as a visual record.
- Make group charts representing learning in a visual form.
- Have surprise tests or a quiz to test movement of knowledge to long-term memory.
- Have groups or individuals present information to the class.
- Use a debate to argue the importance of certain points of view regarding what has been researched. This could include fact and opinion.
- Involve movement such as a relay where participants need to complete a certain number of memory tasks related to the topic. This can be done with simple tasks such as multiplication tables or basic facts to more involved studies.
- Integrate the main points into well-known stories such as *Goldilocks and the Three Bears*.

---

1. Frisbee® is a registered trademark of Wham-O, Inc.

16

Memory Techniques

Expecting students to remember is one thing. Having it actually happen is another. We are designed to forget most things unless they are related to survival issues, are highly emotional, or have a high degree of personal importance (Sprenger, 2003).

Apart from using cues to aid the memory process, we can teach students memory techniques. These techniques are an effort to take something abstract and represent it in a more concrete form (Sprenger, 2003). There are many good techniques available. Some use processes, such as "loci" that have been proven for more than two thousand years!

Review learning after ten minutes, twenty-four hours, and seven days.

SOURCE: Trudeau, 1997

Remember, it is *the brain that does the work that does the learning*. Students need to be actively involved in learning reviews. A wide variety of review techniques will allow a greater possibility of both storage and retention to occur for individuals. Here are some review techniques you can use:

- Sit with a partner and check off three main points on your fingers. Your partner does the same.
- Use the same process to state what you agreed or disagreed with in the past lesson.
- While sitting with a partner, wrap string around your finger as you recap the lesson. The sensation of winding is good for tactile learners.
- Another tactile technique uses a length of thin rope or material. The learner retells main points by tying a series of knots. He then holds each knot in turn and retells the main points to a partner.

- Sit in a circle and pass a ball of wool around. After speaking, each student retains a piece of wool from the ball, and then passes the ball to the next person. In this way a pattern is formed and the teacher can see who has spoken.
- Use parts of the body to "peg" or attach key points that need to be remembered. You do this by "pegging" a strong visual image of that key point to your feet, knees, or other parts of your body. It is best if these visual stimuli are funny, unusual, or able to provoke an emotion. For example, if I needed to remember that the first key point in my speech related to frogs, I might "peg" (attach) a strong visual image of a frog hanging on to my big toe. When I begin the speech, I wiggle my toe and activate the memory. Other key points are attached to other body parts. This technique is often used by public speakers.
- Pegging can also be done to twenty known objects. "One is sun, two is pants . . ." are well known pegs. You may need to read more about this method.
- Use loci, an ancient Roman technique. With this technique, you visualize a room in your house and mentally hang an idea that you want to remember on a familiar piece of furniture. It usually pays to use no more than ten items in each room. This technique can be practiced in the classroom.
- For the loci expert: Use up to one hundred pegs that you can visualize on a well-known journey. This may include mailboxes, traffic lights, etc. This is more suitable for secondary students.
- Weave key information you have learned into a story. Make it humorous, bizarre, or emotional to stimulate memory pattern.
- Use mnemonics, poems, songs, or rhymes that help for remembering specific facts.

We often work against how memory functions. Not only does learning need to be reviewed regularly, but it needs to be done in the right context. Students need to be taught how to manage stress and how to effectively prepare for a test so that long-term learning is the result.

When your students know that there will be a test each week—for example, a list of this week's spelling words—many will cram for it the night before. The test will now only relate to material that is held in short-term memory—information that has been crammed the night before. This information tends to be forgotten once the test is completed.

The test may be passed successfully, but the information is not retained and generally not transferred to real life. Spelling lists often have little effect on accuracy in written expression.

To test movement to long-term memory, the test needs to be unexpected and must include words or information from previous weeks.

How can we retrieve it if we don't know we've received it?

Hamiora was one of the lead characters in a school production, *The Rats of Hamlin*. As the mayor, he had large amounts of script to remember. He had all the attributes of a born actor—loud and expressive voice, great use of timing when presenting his lines, and a real presence on stage.

Two weeks before opening night, cracks began to appear in his confidence. Although he knew his script, at crucial points in the play he began to lose his way. Practice indeed makes permanent, and that is what began to happen. The hesitations and confusion became a fixed habit and reduced his confidence to a dangerously low level. I was left with a young man with failing self-belief just when we needed it the most.

As part of our "Learn to Learn" program for sixth and seventh grade students, we had been studying memory techniques. One of these is called "pegging," where you use a familiar item, such as particular furniture in your house, to hang a new memory on. The students had enjoyed being able to peg up to sixty items into their memory and then compete with each other to see if they could retrieve all of them.

I sat with Hamiora, and we decided to begin by using the pegging technique for the first section of the script that was proving to be a problem. Because of the shortage of time, it was important to start small and achieve a high degree of success. If this worked, I predicted that his confidence would grow and a more positive attitude would make the task much easier.

We walked through the actions and positioning on stage to promote his locational memory until we reached the first point of confusion. We then identified a key word and movement and repeatedly pegged them into his memory. It was important for Hamiora to identify the specific body movement that would work for him, and we tried quite a few possibilities until he identified one that would work. Our goal was that every time he reached a certain position on stage and moved a part of his body in a certain way, the key word came to mind.

We achieved early success, and a big smile spread across his face. After repeated individual practice time, we incorporated it into a full cast rehearsal with continued success. The cast knew the difficulties that he had been experiencing and gave him a spontaneous round of applause. Hamiora's eyes lit up, and he was now ready to confidently move to the next challenging point. These were all pegged in turn, and by show time Hamiora was ready to perform to the very high standards that he was capable of.

He has since gone on to be a very impressive public speaker at the high school level, winning several age grade competitions in both English and Maori language.

SOURCE: Michael A. Scaddan

17

Rough Draft

Most of what we take in is in the form of "rough draft." It may not be accurate to any great degree, because it will be based on the accuracy of previous information stored in our long-term memory, which in turn is altered through perception and our life-filters (Kovalik, 1997).

Also, if material isn't received through our dominant learning styles, it will have difficulty moving in to our immediate memory. We may find the delivery method too difficult or lacking connection with what we already know (Prashnig, 1998; Sprenger, 2003).

Immediate memory is the first memory stage. It is centered in the hippocampus and holds incoming information for as little as fifteen to twenty seconds. If it is important information or a useful skill that we want to retain, it then needs to pass through more filters into our **working memory** (Sprenger, 2003).

Is the information interesting? Can I understand it? Does it fit previous patterns or link to themes of understanding? Could I use it? If these questions are answered in the affirmative, the information is stored, but still for only long enough to complete the task. This is working memory. We use working memory when we cram the night before an exam, with much of the information forgotten as soon as the exam is finished.

It requires sense, meaning, and repetition to move information to permanent long-term memory. Let's imagine that transfer is required. We want to move the event or learning to long-term storage and be certain that it is retained. We need to utilize as many memory pathways as we can to ensure that transfer occurs for a higher percentage of learners. This transfer can be assisted with the following techniques:

- Teaching others. It is possibly the best learning tool of all.
- Reviewing learning with the statements such as, "I understand . . . but I still have a question about . . . ."

- Changing the learning to another form. For example, you may show the theory as a working model.
- Using a timeline to show sequence and flow.
- Using Venn diagrams to show relationships to other topics.
- Developing a hypothesis and exploring it.
- Creating a test. Writing the questions takes a higher level of skill than just answering them.
- Preparing a presentation to the class on your topic.
- Exploring other selected material on your topic that may confirm or challenge your viewpoint.
- Defending a point of view with a partner using only three main points in a time frame of two minutes. Your partner cannot argue while it is your turn, but summarizes your views at the conclusion of your presentation and then gives his or her point of view in the same way.
- Debating a topic. Defending or debating an idea gives opportunity to develop emotional intelligence skills. Because we often have strong attachment to our ideas, it is easy to lower our defense to a personal attack on the opposition. It is important for learners to understand that when they "polish" an idea by defending a point of view, they need to establish a logical argument. This is great practice for the use of "I" rather than "you" messages.

Everything about us is created by memory: Our genes, our actions,
even our feelings of self-worth.

Teaching in England recently gave me an opportunity to introduce memory and review techniques that I had learned in New Zealand. I was employed on a short-term contract teaching a group of sixth grade students for six weeks. They were just about to take their SAT exams, so I was instructed to cram in all the study that I could. In an effort to make sure that they not only remembered the material but accurately understood it, we began a series of review games. At first they could not understand how a game could help them to study, but once I explained to them that the emotional/fun center and the initial memory center of the brain were close together, they really got into it.

A biology lesson consisted of the students going back over their notes and creating questions and answers about microbes. They had to rate the difficulty and award points from one to four for each question. We then had a game show similar to "Jeopardy" with a host, prizes, and music. It lasted for a long time, during which the students remained focused and enthusiastic. Comments after the exercise included, "Miss Robinson, the game show worked. Microbes are really easy!"

SOURCE: Shannon Robinson, elementary teacher in New Zealand and England

18

Elaboration

Although long-term storage may have occurred, the information might not be as accurate as it could be. We now retrieve those memories and begin to test them in a practical sense. In effect we are working like a jeweler with a diamond from the mine. Like with the uncut diamond, we need to "polish" the rough draft to enhance its accuracy. This step needs to be thought about and planned for. It is part of the teaching process and integral to the philosophy of "teach less, teach it better" (Tate, 2004).

Opening the various memory pathways may be the teacher's responsibility.
Polishing the rough draft is a shared responsibility.

The teacher's role is to provide the opportunity and create the state where risks and mistakes can occur (Kovalik, 1997). The student's role is to develop faith in herself so that she will take the opportunities when they are offered.

This polishing process is called elaboration (deBono, 1995; Raffini, 1996). Elaboration is the opportunity for the learner to tie new information to existing knowledge. It involves these activities:

- exploring
- thinking
- questioning
- framing an hypothesis
- experimenting
- making mistakes
- modifying
- drawing conclusions

Elaboration is an opportunity for exploration using multiple intelligence and higher-level thinking. While all subjects provide opportunity for exploration through elaboration, science provides a simple model to begin with. For some reason, maybe because of the history of science itself, mistakes seem to be more easily accepted in science. Is it the way that we approach it? While writing, spelling, and math have a requirement to be correct, science has a need to be challenged and explained. Perhaps it provides a model for other subjects.

Science works on slight changes in the conditions of the experiment every time it is repeated. Other subjects are normally taught through the process of similarity. However, too much similarity creates confusion in the memory pathways. Science explores through the process of identifying both similarity and difference.

This is a vital part of memory retrieval.

Elaboration is not only for exploration. It is also a time to teach students how to **classify** so that understanding and retrieval are easier (deBono, 1995; Frangeheim, 1998; Smith, 2004). It is the difference between developing a tagged filing system versus the continual input of information in a haphazard manner.

Creating classifications for new learning needs to be taught as a conscious, sequential process.

Specific questions need to be asked initially by the teacher to model the process:

- What are the points of similarity between these two pieces of information?
- What are the points of difference?
- How does this relate to what we already know?
- Has this new knowledge changed your thinking and if so, in what way?
- What do you think differently about today than yesterday?" (for review at the end of the day)

These connections, or lack of, can be shown through techniques such as these:

- Creating a simile, analogy, or metaphor to show the link between abstract concepts and reality (Tate, 2004). These can begin in a simple manner and then become more complex. For example, "A pencil is like a pen because they are both used for writing. A pencil is like an apple because they both have a core and a skin."
- Using mind maps, flowcharts, or graphic organizers to show connection through a visual form (Buzan, 1995; Gelb, 1995).
- Maintaining a diary of learning and thoughts.
- Tests or quizzes to highlight what students know.
- Include extension or experimentation areas in your classroom that can be used in a formal or informal basis.

The more that we refine, the more we reveal patterns of similarity and also subtle differences. This aids future retrieval (Dispenza, 2007). Part of the memory storage process is that like is stored with like (Trudeau, 1997). When we go to retrieve the memory, there may be too many similarities and confusion occurs. Examples would be when we first meet twins or how to use the words "there" and "their" accurately. The twins look alike and the words sound alike. Through experience and elaboration, we begin to see through the initial patterns and notice distinct differences. In the case of the twins, it may be in the way each individual twin acts; with the words, it may be a strong recognition that one contains the letter *I* and refers to people.

The brain stores by similarity but retrieves through difference.

At this point in the development of our school culture, we had realized that learning that involved doing and actually "being there" was one of the most powerful ways to capture students' interest and cement meaningful understanding. Each term there was a major experience for sixth and seventh grade students to focus on, which was often related to education outside the classroom. These activities included a ski trip; making and racing go karts; building cardboard boats large enough to carry two people over the "Cardboard Cup" regatta course; as well as week-long camps at Waitomo caves (a series of limestone caves that can be explored and rafted underground); and in alternate years, a week of camping on a small and isolated island off the coast of New Zealand's North Island.

Unfortunately most of these activities did involve financial outlay, and although group fundraising occurred, some of our students struggled to secure the personal funding required.

One of our more challenging students had not paid his fee for the island camp, and as senior school staff we all agreed that this student would really benefit from such an experience. Because the "I Care" philosophy was a driving force in our school culture, his teacher visited his home and secured the funding to enable the student to attend.

It was well worth the effort, as the camping experience formed the basis of a very positive year for the student. We do believe that this particular beginning allowed him the opportunity to learn more about himself both through elaboration of emotionally intelligent experiences and a hands-on program. This was also a very positive way for teachers to gain a deeper understanding of the student's needs, wants, and strengths; and they were also able to form positive relationships with him.

It would have been so easy to have left this student back at school and have justified it in terms of finances and past behavioral problems. Whenever we faced these situations, we would ask questions related to our philosophy that permeated the school:

- If we really care for this student, what should we do?
- How can we make this student more aware that we care, and in this way promote his or her own feelings of self-worth?
- Is our decision made for administration purposes, or is it based on developing people?

SOURCE: Simon Drewery, former Te Puna teacher and now principal of Waihi Central School, New Zealand

19

Repetition

Having an accurate memory is one thing; retrieving it is a totally different process. We have all had the experience of meeting someone who is familiar and yet suddenly we cannot remember his or her name. Why is this?

We store by similarity and retrieve through difference. Linking involves this dual process but also involves five differing memory aisles (Sousa, 2005; Sprenger, 2003):

- **Semantic:** factual memory relating to words and pictures
- **Episodic:** memory related to time, location, and events
- **Emotional:** memory related to strong feelings
- **Conditioned reflex:** an automatic response that has been taught, such as basic facts, times tables, or a learned behavior
- **Procedural:** understanding and memory of processes such as letter writing, tying shoes, or walking

We may have a strong memory of a particular aspect of the person whose name we forgot—for example, his or her face—which is a semantic memory. However, if we see this person in a different place or if there is any change in the circumstances, no matter how slight, it can upset the memory retrieval systems. Maybe this individual is with a different person or wearing different clothes than usual. It may be a different location or time of day from when we normally meet him or her. The smallest thing can confuse the link. The same applies in all learning, and we need to be aware of it as educators.

If any item is taught using only one memory pathway, it is a fragile link and may be lost easily. If we value something that we teach and if we want the memory of it to be retrieved, it needs to be stored in as many pathways as possible. This can be done through repetition but not rote, i.e., repetition of the same subject, but explored purposefully in many different ways (Howard, 2000; Kovalik, 1997; Udall, 1997).

Here are some ways to tap into and strengthen memory pathways:

- Involve **emotion** through fun, music, stories, humor, or period costumes.
- Enhance **episodic memory** by exploring the subject in different parts of the room or unveiling it as a serial on different days. "Last week we left the subject with an important question to answer. Join us today and share in the next exciting episode of . . . ."
- Strengthen **procedural memory** through hands-on exploration or role-play. It can be recorded on flowcharts or by creating models that show sequence.
- Encourage **semantic memory** by involving key words on charts or mind maps and using videos and transparencies.
- **Conditioned response** is improved by associating aroma, music, flash cards, word association, or movement to specific areas to recall key points about the topic.

After the exploration, retrieval can be enhanced through the following types of trigger questions (Sprenger, 2003), which tap into the five memory aisles:

- Emotional: "How did you feel about it?"
- Episodic: "Where were you when the event happened?"
- Procedural: "How can I use it?"
- Semantic: "What do I know about this?"
- Conditioned response: "What do you think about when you hear or see this?"

Practice does not necessarily make perfect but it does make permanent.

20

Themes

To link all of these processes together, teach in themes. The theme is the umbrella, a broad concept under which the curriculum topics fall (Kovalik, 1997; Udall, 1997).

Especially with preadolescent students, themes need to be about people.
They then become a means of promoting understanding of self.

The brain-compatible model described in the introduction illustrates the importance of both a clear philosophy and themes.

"I care for myself" is the first statement in our philosophy, and until we introduced this particular statement, we made little headway. "I care for others, I care for property, and I care for the environment" can only happen when we as individuals understand the concept of caring. This is personal and individual.

Everything must relate back to *us* on a conscious and nonconscious level, for this is how we see and develop understanding of ourselves and our world. Themes can be used to enhance this practice (Udall, 1997).

"Cooperation" is a people-related theme. "Shapes" is not a good theme, but could be a unit as part of a theme. Initially, themes may not be easy to relate to all subjects in the curriculum; with practice, the links become easier and possibly more abstract.

It is preferable to run the theme for a year with every term divided into smaller themes or subthemes (Kovalik, 1997). This provides a continual link to what is already known.

Here are examples of two annual themes—life cycles and survival—and their subthemes:

Life Cycles

EXPLORED THROUGH

Adaptation   *Exploration*   *Extinction*   *Survival*

OR

Survival

EXPLORED THROUGH

Perseverance   *Courage*   *Planning*   *Optimism*

Themes are an exploration of life. In the elementary school they are about simple topics, but as the student grows they can become more abstract. For example, high school themes could span continuums of thought, such as these:

- opportunity/risk
- right/wrong
- fair/unfair
- true/false
- beautiful/ugly

Themes are not about facts. They need to include contestable statements that can be explored and argued (Udall, 1997). This process leads students to the understanding that life is more complex than we might think and that everything is dependent on degrees and circumstances.

Themes can easily involve patterns, rough drafts, elaboration, and repetition to link and polish concepts and to continue upon the journey of self-knowledge. The arts and outdoor education are a great way to explore the human factors related to theme statements. Drama, art, mime, music, and practical problem solving using outdoor experiences involve the use of all nineteen senses, providing a richness of experience rarely experienced in more formal learning processes (Kovalik, 1997).

THE PLANNING PROCESS

Most of our teachers work in teams. To plan a year of themes/topics, they divide the tasks up. The team first brainstorms the themes and topics. Then the team splits—one of the teachers gathers resources, another establishes the curriculum strands and skill development, while a third records and ties it all together through a mind map. One evening of work completes the core planning for a year! The team approach involves brainstorming and links to past knowledge and experiences. It is its own theme in action and is highly successful.

How we link is how we think.

BRAIN-BASED REVIEW

Doing this at the end of each session, at the end of the day, and at the beginning of the next day ensures that the cycle is well covered.

How successful have you been at incorporating review into your programs on a regular basis? Remember that it will take time to do it successfully, but if you do not create time for reviews to happen, then the foundation for future learning is not established.

Experts have been defined as those who are willing to repeat the same essentials every day. Anthony Robbins (1991) has a favorite saying that "repetition is the mother of skill" (p. 402). To help you succeed in establishing any new practice, it may be a good idea to keep a journal. You might like to record information such as the following:

1. The reviews or new practice that you planned to use that day

2. The reviews that you actually used

3. What the results were

4. The cumulative effect of using them throughout the week

Record success, mistakes, and modifications and regularly read the journal to see your own learning journey.

Habits are not changed in an instant. Many people suggest that twenty-one to thirty days is the time that it takes to change your own behaviors, and that during this time frame there will be mistakes, moments of frustration, and possibly a desire to give up. To ensure success, it is beneficial that you continue to have a reflective partner who can help you think, plan, and develop. Hopefully you can do the same for them.

PART III

Promoting Understanding

A MODEL FOR A "LEARN TO LEARN" FRAMEWORK

As we understand ourselves, so we can understand others (Burns, 1993). Much of what the traditional education system covers does little to assist with self-knowledge (Scaddan, 2002). Self-knowledge is vital so that individuals can learn to motivate themselves, rather than asking the question, "Why should I?" (Harmin, 1998)

This developmental process should not be left to chance (Gordon, 1995). I believe that a sequential, schoolwide program is best; but if that cannot happen, the process can take place in an individual classroom (Jensen, 2006).

The classroom teacher cannot provide all the opportunities to cater for individual learning styles and learning needs. Instead, a program needs to be developed in which students acquire self-knowledge and are then encouraged and obliged to use this knowledge to assist their own learning, while at the same time developing responsibilities so that the rights of other learners are not compromised (Costa & Kallick, 2000; Prashnig, 1996, 1998).

This is higher-level thinking in action.

Here is an overview of the program developed at Te Puna School, with more detail provided in the tools that follow. It is designed to be sequential, but overlaps to cater for new students entering at later grades.

- In kindergarten, five- and six-year-olds are involved in an initial program introducing them to some factors involved with their learning. That first step concentrates on creating an understanding of how we take in information, which is initially through our five senses. Also covered are the support factors for effective learning: the need for sleep, exercise, water, healthy food, and love. Throughout the program, accelerated learning techniques are used to create strong memory. This includes movement, songs, poems, simple experiments, and discussion.
- Our seven- and eight-year-olds are introduced to simple facts about the brain, such as the left side of the brain operating the right side of the body, the role of the lobes, and the concept of learning styles. I use a lot of props for this, such as a large nose clip to show olfactory (smell) learning and large ears to indicate auditory. Again, I use songs that are linked to well-known tunes to help to get the learning to "stick."
- By the time students are nine or ten, they are establishing a stronger view of themselves. This is when we introduce them to the concept of learning styles and learning conditions. This is a self-analysis, but is now based on experience and reflection regarding learning preferences. We provide both students and parents with a series of tools. This program took us six years of trial and mistakes, those wonderful learning situations followed by constant modification. The current program is not only very student-based, but involves the wider family. It runs over a two-year time frame.

- At ten and eleven years of age, the concept of multiple intelligences is introduced. This component is designed primarily to improve self-worth and is run on a two-year basis.
- Our twelve- and thirteen-year-olds are introduced to "The Twenty Rules of the Game of School and How to Play It." This is a ten-week program, developed for our seventh grade students, in which two rules are explored each week. These are the unwritten rules that are rarely discussed, but are the backbone for success in school and in life. They are woven through a theme of memory techniques, time-management skills, speed reading, exam techniques, and self-belief. Many stories are used as metaphors, along with a wide variety of accelerated and brain-compatible techniques.
- All levels begin the first lesson with a review of what has been taught before so that the strong link is maintained. This helps to introduce new students to the process. Students are encouraged to use the correct terminology and to keep learning diaries.
- This particular program emphasizes the skills required for academic learning as well as emotional intelligence (EQ). Students are provided with a wide range of opportunities to practice these skills and are encouraged to modify them for their own particular needs.

Self-knowledge is the true journey of life.

21

Input Through Learning Styles

A learning style is how we input information before we begin the task of processing (Jensen, 2006; Prashnig; 1996; Sprenger, 2003). In real life there may be no perceivable gap between these processes unless the task is new or difficult.

There are many models you can use as a basis for teaching the concept of learning styles. In the Dunn and Dunn (1994) model that we use, there are six preferences for learning styles. We use all of them to varying degrees, but some, depending on the individual, will be more dominant.

Of these preferences, four are classified as major:

- **Visual:** Visual learners prefer readings, videos, posters, computer screens, and other images. They often need visual instructions, including written notes and gestures. A common comment may be, "Look on the board, it's written up there!"
- **Auditory:** People with an auditory learning style prefer lectures, audio-tapes, and discussion. They can listen to instructions and repeat them. A common comment is, "Didn't you hear what she said?"
- **Kinesthetic:** Kinesthetic learners prefer hands-on activities, movement, and active learning. These people are frequent "touchers" and like to stand close to you when they talk. They often "follow the herd" when it comes to instructions and may ask, "What are we meant to be doing?"
- **Tactile:** Students with a tactile learning style use small motor control and fiddle a lot in class. They prefer to learn by manipulating materials and are often very sequential. Once they are involved in a task, they are oblivious to instructions unless the material they are working on is removed. In recent times many educators consider this to be the fourth major learning style.

The remaining two learning styles are considered **minor** because few of us use them as our dominant primary input:

- **Olfactory:** Smell is the only sense that has direct access to the brain's sensory systems. It is primarily there for survival purposes; this is why we often smell our food and react strongly to foul odors. It has a subliminal effect on learning and can be enhanced with the subtle use of aromas in the classroom.
- **Gustatory (taste):** These learners input through the lips and mouth. They are often seen sucking their pencil, hair, or clothing and touching their lips or sucking their fingers while thinking.

By the time learners are about eight years old, we find it beneficial for them to be more aware of how they learn and whether they have developed strong preferences for any areas.

Not long after implementing this tool, we realized that we were running the risk of classifying students into learning boxes. We were literally saying, "Those who prefer to learn visually, come over here. Those who prefer kinesthetic learning, move over there." This created a narrow, rather than expansive, learning environment.

Reflection and a revised focus led us to provide a wider range of experiences for all to participate in, while acknowledging that some would prefer certain input styles. As much as possible we factored a degree of choice. As students consciously learned through a range of styles, they were able to become more flexible in their approaches and developed a deeper understanding of themselves.

Imagine life if we were all the same!

> Some of us learn with our hands,
>
> and others learn with our eyes.
>
> Our body, ears, nose, and mouth
>
> all help to make us wise.
>
> There is no way that's "learning right."
>
> No way that's "learning wrong."
>
> But we need to know what's right for us,
>
> so we can move along.
>
> This poem is part of our learning styles and conditions analysis and is used as an introduction and reminder that we are all unique.
>
> SOURCE: Michael A. Scaddan

22

Learning Preferences

There are certain conditions that will have a positive or negative impact on us as learners (Dryden & Voss, 2001; Ginnis, 2002; Jensen, 2005). Again there are many models that you can explore, but the learning preferences remain fairly standard. Following our work with senses and learning styles, we developed a simple questionnaire related to fifteen learning preferences. These were based upon Dunn and Dunn's (1994) model. This included questions about preferences regarding the following issues:

- global or sequential processing
- four major learning styles
- need for snacks/water
- movement possibilities
- work time
- noise levels
- lighting
- temperature
- seating arrangements
- group or individual working/learning conditions
- independence
- perseverance
- authority
- motivation
- structure of the working environment

We initially began by listing these factors and then developing a questionnaire for students to answer during their fourth year of school. The results were not what we wanted. In many cases we found that students either randomly chose an answer or, more often, gave us the answer that they thought we wanted to hear.

As a result, we developed a two-year program that explored the fifteen learning conditions. Two learning conditions were studied each term of the four-term year, with learning styles and global/sequential covered every year. The next step provided an exciting breakthrough.

Instead of just having a questionnaire, staff devised an exposure system in which all students experienced a variety of learning conditions, allowing them to develop insight into their own learning requirements.

For example, if we were looking at how the students related to **noise** factors, a five-week exposure was developed with students rating each experience as to how it affected them.

- **Week 1**. During a spelling test the **lawn mower was left running** outside the classroom window.
- **Week 2**. The test was done **in absolute silence**.
- **Week 3**. The **teacher talked** during the test.
- **Week 4**. **Heavy metal music** was played.
- **Week 5**. A selection of **baroque music** was played as a background to the test.

Students then **reviewed their ratings and ranked them from positive to negative** in regard to how they felt various noises affected them. Many were surprised that the results were different from what they expected. Some were oblivious to noise, while others were strongly influenced.

This was followed with a series of tools being given to the students about different music that may assist their learning (Miles, 1997). This included the opportunity to wear earplugs or old headphones at certain times during class, as well as the development of quiet times and places. Also, the student's self analysis and additional tools were shared with parents through discussion and as part of the student's learning portfolio.

With two preferred conditions covered each term, the fifteen factors were covered over two years. Older students were encouraged to review these conditions, annually rating themselves on a continuum. This then became a continual self-review of how they currently prefer to learn and hints as to what they could do if conditions were not ideal for them.

If we all preferred the same conditions, where would we live?

23

Multiple Intelligences

In our experience, many learners pass through the schooling system with poor self-esteem. Some of this comes as a result of external factors, but some is a result of what we often regard as intelligence (Dryden & Voss, 2001).

Traditional testing normally concentrates on two intelligences: linguistic, the intelligence that reflects how well you read, spell, and write; and math/logical, which is the math, science, and problem-solving intelligence (Buzan, 2000; Pink, 2003).

Many educational systems throughout the world are currently concentrating development in areas of literacy, numeracy, and technology. Very few people would debate their importance. However, viewed from a multiple-intelligence perspective, this is a very narrow approach to lifelong learning. In addition, if you have no great ability in these areas, you may be seen or see yourself as an educational failure (Goleman, 2006; Jensen, 2006).

Intelligence is broader than that: In the last twenty-five years, there has been an enormous amount of research related to intelligence. Some notable developments include the following:

- Howard Gardner's (1983, 1999) theory of multiple intelligences (MI).
- David Goleman's (1996) views on the importance of emotional intelligence including attitude, persistence, and relationships.
- Al Gore's comments regarding the value of distributed intelligence. This particular intelligence is defined as the ability to assemble knowledge and solve problems using a wide range of sources including other people.

Understanding intelligence forms the fourth part of our "Learn to Learn" program and continues the theme about understanding yourself.

This process is taught to ten- and eleven-year-olds and, at this stage, provides teachers with a framework for planning and assessment procedures. Its main focus is to emphasize to students that there are many forms of intelligence, some of which they will be strong at and others less so. However, they also learn that intelligences can be developed with concentration and perseverance and can decline if skills are neglected, even for a short period of time.

We based this program on Gardner's (1999) definitions of eight intelligences. Other intelligences—such as spiritual, streetwise, moneymaking, and technological—have been explored by some researchers and could be included if appropriate, but were not part of our core model. Our model focused on these intelligences:

- **Intrapersonal:** how well we understand ourselves
- **Interpersonal:** how well we relate to others
- **Linguistic:** the ability to read, write, and spell
- **Math/logical**: the ability to solve problems and think in a sequential and orderly manner
- **Visual/spatial**: the ability to perceive relationships of size and distance, locate compass directions, read maps, and manipulate three-dimensional images
- **Musical:** the ability to play, sing, make instruments, compose, harmonize, and conduct
- **Kinesthetic**: the ability to coordinate one's body using strength, speed, and grace
- **Naturalistic:** the ability to understand where we are in time and space and an affinity with plants and animals, conservation, and ecology

It is not interest in a subject that defines the intelligence. Instead, it is the understanding that we all have some talent throughout these areas and in certain areas, we have capacity for greater skill.

Each of the intelligences has many subsections (Gardner, 1983). For example, in music we may be able to read music as well as play several instruments, but we may struggle to sing in tune, compose, conduct, or build instruments.

In our "Learn to Learn" program, four intelligences are targeted each year. Each intelligence is defined and then explored through a variety of activities. Students build a graph of the areas in which they have strengths; the teacher often assists in this assessment.

The MI model is then reinforced through the parallel processes of assessment and parent conferences to build a mutual understanding of the concepts among all parties. Parents, students, and teachers need to realize that abilities are wide-ranging and that nothing is simple until you can do it.

We are all both gifted and disabled learners.

BRAIN-BASED REVIEW

Our "Learn to Learn" program was schoolwide and run by one person—in our case, me as the principal. This gave me an opportunity to model teaching practice as well as get to know the students. Our program was based on a sequence of skills and knowledge development that was an essential part of the "I Care" philosophy. If you are planning this type of program in your class or school, these questions should be helpful:

1. Who will be the personnel involved?

2. What resources do you currently have and what resources will you need to acquire for this program to be effective?

3. At what level will you begin the program in the school and how much time—in hours, days, or weeks—would you plan for each level?

4. How will your program transfer to classroom practice?

5. Will the teachers have follow-up lessons to complete?

6. Will input lessons be cyclic or in a single block?

7. How will you review the program?

8. Will you assess the effects of the program, and if so, how?

24

Motivators

How we motivate ourselves to take action is one of the keys for long-term success (Canfield, 2005; Kraus, 2002; Smith, 2004). As part of the development of life skills, we explore some of the factors that have been identified as life's motivators. Each of us experiences all of these factors, but as individuals we value them in differing degrees. These are the needs that drive us, the causes of our actions and reactions in life (Raffini, 1996; Reiss, 2000; Robbins, 1996).

We used the following model of motivational factors:

1. **Survival:** This is the number-one need in life. Under the umbrella of survival, we do everything in life to gain pleasure and avoid pain. Of these two, the biggest is our desire to avoid pain, because pain has a strong connection to our physical and emotional well being. This is the trigger for the "flight and fight" syndrome discussed earlier in Tool 5.

2. **Fun:** This is a strong motivator for many people. These people are always looking for the humorous side of life. Class clowns, practical jokers, and joke tellers may have a very high need for fun. They are easily bored and often cause disruption in class until they understand their own needs.

3. **Power:** A person who is motivated by power enjoys achievement, goal setting, and relishes new challenges. This is the motivation to have power over yourself, rather than power over others. Because of this, it is quite a subtle concept to teach younger students.

4. **Freedom:** People who have a strong need for freedom are the rule breakers. They question authority and ask, "Why should I?" They resent being ordered around and told what to do. They respond well to choice, requests, and being given the reason "why" before the task is given.

5. **Love and connection:** For some people, love and connection are their prime motivators. These are individuals who love friends, meeting new

people, talking, and mixing. They dislike being alone and will often break the silence with a whispered conversation.

6. **Self-worth:** If survival is the beginning, self-worth is the goal, the life's journey. If we do not achieve a satisfactory measure of it, life is unpleasant and frustrating (Glasser, 1998; Rogers, 2003).

If you imagine a bull's eye with three concentric circles, survival is the inner one, the next four motivators rotate throughout the middle circle, and self-worth is the outer circle (Scaddan, 2002).

HOW TO TEACH STUDENTS ABOUT MOTIVATORS

Through experience we found that students are able to begin to understand some of these concepts from the age of ten to twelve years. For ease of understanding, the program concentrated on four motivators, leaving survival and self-worth for later study.

To introduce the motivators to students I developed the following framework that you may find useful:

- Create a folder of sixty to one hundred photos, sufficient for a class of up to thirty students. These can be cut out of magazines or found on the Internet.
- Each photo will be of a scene, an activity, a creature or plant, groups of people, or animals in various situations.
- Spread the photos on the floor and allow students to choose two that really interest them. If time permits they can discuss these with the teacher on an individual basis. If not, have them talk about their choices with a partner.
- Ask the students to identify some adjectives to describe the pictures.
- List the adjectives that they have used under the four motivator headings.
- The students' choices, coupled with the words they use to describe them, will give an indication as to which motivators are the most important in their lives.
- I then have them rank the four factors on a bar graph as a visual way for them to see the individual mix of their motivators. This then provides an explanation for why they make certain choices in life and why some experiences are more enjoyable than others.
- We then look specifically at the learning tasks that they enjoy and the ones that are less desirable and see if the pattern is constant. If not, the graph can be adjusted.
- These graphs are useful self-knowledge as to why we make certain choices in life.

There is only one person in life who I can change.

When our twelve- and thirteen-year-old students assessed their own "life motivators," the results were surprising. At this time in their lives, students are often beginning to reject their parents and siblings, yet more than eighty-five percent of our students chose "Love and Connection" as being most important.

It is easy to forget that all of us need other people, and this is especially so during the turbulent teenage years. When the group reflected on their choices, students were able to discuss their reasons openly and with depth. That discussion led into a talk about the effects of the break-up of families and death of grandparents and other family members.

Many shared that not only was a family breakup emotionally difficult, but that it created organizational problems. One particular issue occurred if students went to see their mothers or fathers outside the "family home" either for nights during the week or on the weekend. This created organizational and time management issues. As young teenagers, they had to remember to pack their clothes needed for the next day and to think of all of the issues related to home learning. What resources were at the other house? Was there a place to study? Did they remember their books and other such issues? Boys seemed to find these management skills particularly difficult with the result that school work often suffered.

Everyone agreed that it was very stressful even without the complication of separated parents and new family set-ups.

SOURCE: Michael A. Scaddan

25

Four Great Questions

Questions help us gain understanding for better decision making (Kraus, 2002). Following understanding of the six motivational factors, these four questions (Glasser, 1998) formed one of the cornerstones of our school-wide counseling program:

    1. What do you want?

    2. What are you doing to get it?

    3. Is it working?

    4. What is your plan?

Notice that three of these questions begin with "what." We soon found that asking the "why" for behavior was a waste of time. We are often unaware and give little conscious thought to our behavior. Asking the "why" frequently led to an "I don't know" response (Robbins, 1996). This was frustrating for the adult and child and was a stalemate situation.

It is important that as the teacher you provide the "why," but follow with a "what" question.

Asking these four questions fit in well to our philosophy of "I care." It was also a powerful way to teach students to take responsibility for their own lives. Once a person understands his unique mix of motivators, he can understand the "why" behind the "want."

These questions form part of Glaser's (1998) "reality therapy." During the counseling process, the onus is on the student to take responsibility by answering the four questions.

There is no opting out. If the "What do you want?" question is asked and the answer is "Don't know," the teacher continues to probe. "I don't understand what 'don't know' means. Is it that you have never thought about it? If so let's think now. What do you want?"

HOW TO USE THESE QUESTIONS WITH STUDENTS

- These questions can be used in class with the whole group; if they are used for counseling, it needs to take place in private and be confidential.
- Take time to greet and reestablish relationships. Statements such as "Thanks for coming" work well.
- If the student has requested the session, ask what he or she hopes to get from it; if you have requested the session, say what you hope to achieve.
- Explain that as part of the process, you will be exploring the four questions.
- Using humor in this process helps to break down barriers. Establishing a good relationship between the teacher and the student is vital.
- Tell stories about how others have achieved what they wanted in similar circumstances. This may include your own personal stories.
- The idea is to replace a top-down model with one that encourages students to think about what they want, what their motivators are, and their degrees of success in achieving them.
- Establish a "where to now" plan and ask, "How will you know when you have achieved what you want?"
- Schedule a time for a review meeting.

If the student says that she wants to continue to misbehave, carefully explain the consequences that will occur. If she continues to press for them, follow the process through. It may be a journey that she needs to experience.

If you don't know where you are going, you will certainly get there.

26

WIIFM

We have talked before about students developing internal motivation and understanding about themselves. We also know that for higher level thinking to develop, "What's in it for me" (WIIFM) is a very strong motivator (Canfield, 2005; Rogers, 2003; Rose & Nicholl, 1997).

The teacher can assist by keeping this in mind when planning and teaching units. Some of these items should be present in all learning experiences and a variety provided over the year (Ginnis, 2002; Harmin, 1998; Pinker, 1997; Politano & Paquin, 2000).

These "buy in" factors relate strongly to our six motivators.

This list is the result of a ten-year study of brain-compatible learning in action:

- Is a clear "why" provided for the experience?
- Are there clear expectations of what will be learned, how it will be learned, and how learners will know when they have learned it?
- Is there a real-life opportunity to use the skill or learning?
- Does it include survival-based factors, e.g., personal challenges, outdoor pursuits, or situations involving risk?
- Is it innovative?
- Does it have a strong appeal to the senses (e.g., unusual textures, exotic foods)?
- Does it build on current knowledge and experience?
- Does it include safe learning processes such as rituals, repetition, or the practice of previously learned skills?
- Does it have an appeal to individuals regardless of age, gender, experiences, or culture?
- Does it include meaningful problem solving?

- Does it include movement or hands-on learning?
- Is there an element of fun or humor?
- Is there opportunity for a flexible approach, such as doing worksheet questions in any order?
- Is there a variety of learning style experiences involved?
- Can the learning be shown through a range of intelligences?
- Does it contain aspects of competitiveness?
- Is it cooperative, with opportunities for group or partner work?
- Is there opportunity for individual work?
- Does it relate to personal goals?
- Does it contain a perceived advantage or benefit?
- Is there possibility for skill or knowledge enhancement?
- It is achievable within the given time frame?
- Are resources available?
- Will it involve satisfaction both during the task and at completion?
- Are there clear mini-steps to measure success?
- Does it involve a contribution to society at class level or beyond? (Frankl, 2004)

Note that some of these factors appear to contradict themselves. That is because all learners are unique and therefore motivational factors will vary. To cope, the teacher needs to remember this:

Choice and variety are the cornerstones of learning.

27

Pulling Your Own Strings

They made me do it." "She made me mad." "It's not my fault." These are comments I heard many times during my career, both from students and adults. But we need to be clear that no one can control your life unless you let them (Dyer, 1977; Robbins, 1996). This is one of the most important messages I have learned and one that I continually pass on to others.

In my office is a great big marionette—a puppet on strings. This is one of the most frequently used pieces of brain equipment that I have. I used to draw the puppet but I find having one that people can manipulate is much better.

I begin by telling stories about my own life when I have let people make me angry. I tell one particular story where a girl regularly teased me about having a girlfriend. I would get very angry with her. (By this time the puppet is jiggling wildly.)

One day when I was ten, I decided that I knew what to do. I would make her angry instead. I retaliated with the comment, "That's OK. You've got a boyfriend." I remember standing there so satisfied, much like a boxer who has just hit his opponent and is waiting for the knockdown.

Instead the girl replied, "That's true, and his name is Ron!" I was left speechless.

From my desk I then take out a large pair of scissors and pretend to cut the strings above the puppet, while relating that I tried to control her, but she neatly cut the strings. This is when I began to learn that I needed to control my own puppet rather than letting others control me.

I then ask, "Do you want (such and such) to control you?"

The answer is always, "No."

"Well then," I ask, "How can you cut the strings?"

We then brainstorm suggestions, including how and when they can be used. I used the following procedures to ensure success:

- I remind the person that I have been trying to cut strings for most of my life and that it is sometimes still quite a challenge.
- The scissors and the cutting process need to be visualized as soon as you feel loss of control; this may need to be repeated many times over a short period.
- It needs to be worked on regularly, but when you succeed, and you will, you will feel so good because you are in control of yourself. Practice makes permanent.
- Finally, we need to be aware of times that we try to pull other people's strings and eliminate that.
- Use the puppet at school assemblies, class meetings, and staff meetings on a regular basis.
- It is great to involve assistants in the role-play and use real-life stories to illustrate the concept.

This is truly about "I care for myself."

It amazes me how many adults do not understand this concept. As a result we have families, businesses, and some schools using practices based upon guilt and emotional blackmail. These are both crippling and nonproductive. Teaching this process to staff and parents is equally important and is a vital part of the journey to self-knowledge.

People can only take control of your life if you give them permission.

28

Goal Setting

Pulling your own strings" involves taking responsibility for your own life. Goal setting can be part of this process. A lot is said about goal setting, but much needs to be understood before it will work successfully (Canfield, 2005; Covey, 2004; Kraus, 2002).

- Students need to understand that a goal is a target. Relating the word to sports and real life is essential. I have talked to students who use the word "goal" but have no idea what it really means (Canfield & Hansen, 2000).
- Goals are about little steps. We nonconsciously set goals all the time; if we didn't, we wouldn't get up in the morning. It is a matter of making them conscious and realizing that we are all capable of success (Buzan, 2001).
- Goals need to be set by the individual, although some assistance may be required. When another person creates goals for you to achieve, there is little chance of success (Frankl, 2004).
- Most students operate in what is known as "in time." In other words, they operate in the here and now. Many goals are long-term with no specific steps to begin the process. At this age, a long-term time frame is doomed to failure (Secunda, 1999).
- Goals that we set and do not achieve can be self-destructive. The act of incompletion is generally negative and has the possibility of promoting poor self-belief and or learned helplessness (Buzan, 2001).
- Keeping goals short-term and simple reduces the risk of failure (Secunda, 1999). Practice by having a daily ritual during which you tell the students about the goals:

What they are expected to learn

How they will be allowed to learn it

How they will know when they have learned it

How they will be able to use it

Goals need to be **SMARTY:**

Specific: General statements are too vague. What do you actually want?

Measurable: How will you know when you have achieved them? Have you incorporated success criteria that you can measure on the way?

Active: Goals need commitment. You will need to do something to achieve them.

Realistic: With your current situation, skills, and connections, is the goal realistic?

Timely: Is this the best time to commit yourself to this course of action?

Yours: Personal goals are more likely to motivate and be achieved.

Goals always need to be stated in the positive (see Tool 29). They are more effective if they are related to attitude, time management, and work habits—issues that the learner can control.

At the end of the day, or the end of each session, some time needs to be devoted to reflection:

- Did the students achieve their goals and, if so, to what degree?
- Were there any circumstances that assisted the achievement process?
- Can these conditions be created again?
- Were there circumstances that worked against the goal achievement?
- How could these be avoided in the future?
- What is the next step to take?

This process can be done in written or oral form, in small groups, with a peer or individually. We now have students taking responsibility for their own learning and a loop being completed. Remember to have goal-free days as a novelty. If continued without a break, rituals risk becoming boring.

*Life is a journey, but it is even more spectacular if you have
some idea of what you want to experience on the way.*

We were spending a session on goal setting as part of our senior school "Learn to Learn" program. One boy in particular, whose name was Tamati, was having difficulty on deciding a short-term, but important goal for the next few weeks. Tamati was very tall and spoke with a mumbling style, two points that proved to be significant. By the end of the session, he still did not have a goal. I shared with him that unless we were able to set one soon, I felt that we may have missed an opportunity.

(Continued)

(Continued)

> While all of this was happening, I was putting the finishing touches to a script for the senior show. For maximum participation opportunity, I always involve two full casts, including a doubling up of all main characters. The show for that year was an updated version of *Gulliver's Travels,* so I needed two tall students to play Gulliver.
>
> Tamati met me a couple of days after our goal setting session and said that he had decided on what he wanted.
>
> "That's great," I replied. "What is it?"
>
> "I want to audition for the main part. I want to be Gulliver."
>
> My heart dropped. Here was a boy whose speech was unclear because of the way that he mumbled, and he wanted the main part. What was I going to say? Luckily, something stopped me from giving him a negative reply. Instead I accepted his goal and gave him a part of the script to learn for the audition.
>
> At the first audition he was terrible! Not only did he mumble, but he lost his place, missed his cues and didn't know his words. Hoping for success, we persevered, but over the next few weeks very little positive change occurred. I had to make a decision to retain him or remove him from the cast. I delayed as long as possible, giving him every opportunity to reach his goal. Finally, a few days before the dress rehearsal, he got a few lines correct—clearly stated and with the tone I wanted. I remember being so pleased and showed it by giving the young giant a hug. Would he get there?
>
> On the production nights he was superb, revealing a dry sense of humor, great acting, and a clear voice. His parents, myself, and of course Tamati himself were thrilled. I shared the story of my doubts and his success in front of the school assembly and at conferences in Europe. None of this would have happened if I had made the decision as to what he was able to dream.
>
> SOURCE: Michael A. Scaddan

29

"Myffirmations"

The subconscious mind is not designed to judge what is true and what is false. Instead, it accepts any information that is put into it, especially if it is regularly received (Kehoe, 1998).

This means that your self-talk is incredibly important (Buzan, 2001; DePorter, 1992; Dryden & Voss, 2001). It is estimated that as we enter our teenage years, our own thoughts are our biggest source of negative input and that we use negative to positive at a rate of six to one! When you consider that we have thirty-five thousand to sixty thousand thoughts per day, it is no wonder that some people have lives filled with depression, trauma, and disappointment (Parker, 1993).

To try to encourage more positive attitudes, our school was turned into a "Put-Up Zone." Initially, we placed signs around the school and in classes saying "No Put-Downs" (Kaufeldt, 2001). They had little effect; then we realized that we were stating what we wanted in the negative.

The signs were replaced with the more positive "Put-Up Zone" and an associated rule was put into place. It was a rule because it related to people's mental health (see Tool 3). If anybody was heard making a put-down statement to herself or others, she was required to state two compliments, known as "put-ups."

The staffroom was the most difficult place to change.

Put-downs and sarcasm are similar in that some people use them as a form of humor. Unfortunately, they are never funny to the receiver. Sarcasm is an extremely stress-provoking form of communication because the recipient is always left in doubt as to the truthfulness of the comment (Sapolsky, 1998). Did he mean it or was he joking?

Sarcasm never strengthens a relationship.

Put-downs are more obvious because their intent is clear. Put-downs are clearly negative in form. Their objective is to boost the ego of the person who delivers them. Recent research, however, confirms that they negatively affect both the giver and receiver, elevating stress levels and lowering the immune system. They are incredibly destructive (Dyer, 2004). Therefore, to enhance goal setting and make our own lives better, it is beneficial to be positive with both our thoughts and words.

After all, what is the point in setting a goal and then saying that you won't achieve it?

This constantly positive and reinforcing self-talk is essential. Often referred to as affirmations, we labeled them "myffirmations" or "Iffirmations," terms used to establish a personal link in an effort to increase motivation and to reinforce that they are about and for the benefit of you.

Myffirmations prepare the mind to encourage the event to happen. It is like preparing the garden before you plant the seeds. There are some simple rules of usage (Buzan, 2001):

- **Aim for what you want, rather than what you want to avoid.** "I must stop failing science tests" concentrates on the word "failing." It is better to affirm, "I always prepare for and achieve great results in my tests."
- **Tell the truth.** When you make the affirming statement, it must be something that you can believe.
- **Remain positive.** Negative or unattractive thoughts create tension.
- **Be clear about what you want.** "I want to work faster" is very vague and may happen, but with the negative spin of increased speed resulting in careless errors. Instead affirm, "I am making my time management more effective and achieving greater results."
- **Make your myffirmations strong.** Words like "want," "need to," and "try" are wishful thinking. "I will" is another delaying myffirmation because it means that it will happen some other time. Instead, use words such as "already," "capable," "able," "learning," or "successfully achieving."
- **Include "ing" words to promote action and truthfulness.** These words can also assist in combating guilt. Here are some examples:
  - "Every day in every way I am getting better and better."
  - "I am increasingly able to make great decisions."
  - "I am becoming fitter and healthier."

Imagine it, make your thoughts vivid, and the event will unfold.

30

Overviews

If we want students to value learning, they need to be actively involved in it. For this to happen, they need to know clearly where they are heading and what is expected from them (Blanchard & Johnson, 1996; Jensen, 2005). Without a clear target, perseverance will be limited and outcomes vague (Buzan, 2001). A vital part of this guiding process is to provide an overview so that clear expectations are shared (Smith, 2004). I recommend these four overview questions:

- What am I expected to learn?
- How will I be able to learn it?
- How will I know when I have been successful?
- How will I be able to use it?

Too often, learners operate in a vacuum without fully understanding what is required of them. Global learners in particular—and this is applicable to many males—require the full picture before they can proceed (Prashnig, 1998). An overview at the beginning of the day with more specifics before each session is an important part of teacher planning.

A large part of the overview, especially with older students, is being able to provide the "why" for the experience. This is more effective if it is given first (Allen, 2002). For example, the teacher may start the day by saying something like, "As a result of yesterday's learning we need to review the following points . . . " or "Because the Romans had a major influence on how our school system developed, we are going to study them next week."

Overviews can be given orally, but are even more effective if they are reinforced with visual forms, such as those listed below, to cater for other learning styles (Prashnig, 1998):

- overhead transparencies
- PowerPoint

- notes on a whiteboard
- charts
- art work
- posters
- mind maps
- graphic organizers

OVERVIEW GUIDELINES

- Begin with the "why," followed by keyword statements about the next session. Allow time for questions and short discussion (Fogarty, 2002).
- Allow some choice for how students will learn during the session (Kaufeldt, 2001) and their learning objectives (Raffini, 1996).
- Have students maintain "goal diaries" so they can see how far they have come as well as where they are going (Raffini, 1996).
- In order to maintain connection to previous learning, it is beneficial to retain the previous day's overview on display (Kaufeldt, 1999). This allows students who were absent to focus on what they missed and allows other learners to constantly review. It is also an important indicator of how well learning in your class links between the known and the new.
- Examples of successful learning—such as completed assignments, detailed mind maps, or detailed art forms—are also beneficial to have on display. These can be supported with statements that reveal the marking criteria. "For a pass, your work will include . . . . For a credit, it also will need to include the following details . . . ; and for a distinction, this is what I will be looking for . . . ."
- Plan reflection time for students to identify what they have learned. Rubrics, mind maps, and graphic organizers are useful reflective tools (Fogarty, 2002).
- To remind yourself of the need for overviews, reflect on the "Four Questions" as you are planning. You may find it beneficial to have them displayed in the room as a chart. This will provide a constant visual reminder to you as a teacher.

Do less, do it better.

BRAIN-BASED REVIEW

Many of these last tools are concerned with self-development. Teaching should always involve learning and learning should always involve teaching. For me, a lesson that I always learn when assisting students is about the need to cut the puppet strings. It is a life-long journey. The following review questions are here to stimulate your thinking about your own journey:

1. While working through these tools, have you noticed a change in your own attitude to the learning process? If so, what are the changes?

2. Which tools do you feel the most comfortable using?

3. Which tools do you still feel uncomfortable with? Maybe this is not the time to deal with them, or maybe that feeling of being uncomfortable is your personal growth signal. It is often through the biggest challenges that we learn the most.

4. How are your plans developing for a "Learn to Learn" program?

5. I used a range of photos for the "Life's Motivators" activities. I'm sure that you have already begun your collection. What other photos are you looking for at this stage?

6. I use the list of WIIFM factors as a reminder when I'm planning work. Are there additions that you have made to these?

7. If you had to rate the five best tools that you have used so far, what would they be?

8. Who can you find to share your successes with?

ACHIEVEMENT DATA

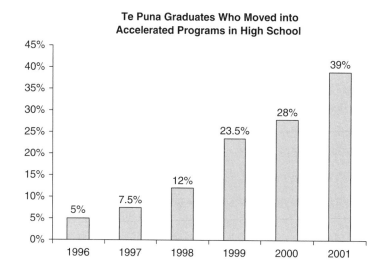

Te Puna Graduates Who Moved into Accelerated Programs in High School

These graphs relate to our graduates moving into the high school program. Based upon our roll figures, approximately five percent of our graduates should have gained entry to advanced programs in middle school and high school. From 1996 to 2001, we moved significantly above this mark. The graph does not continue beyond 2001 because the high schools significantly changed their data entry processes so that we were no longer able to use comparative figures.

These results truly indicate the effect of brain-compatible programs on academic achievement. The significant changes are due to many factors, but central to this success is the fact that students were able to take more control of their own destinies as a result of understanding themselves, how they were motivated, and how they learned.

This in turn altered their images of their capabilities, with the result that more and more realized that they could achieve at a higher level.

This academic performance was not confined to our graduates. In New Zealand the literacy mark is based on the percentage of students who read and understand text at or above the average level for their chronological age. The average throughout the country is eighty percent, and it is this benchmark that is used as a national guideline. In 2004, ninety-seven percent of our girls and ninety-three percent of our boys surpassed this benchmark. The boys' figure is especially significant as throughout the nation, boys' achievement is falling rather than progressing.

What are not shown on any of these graphs are the figures for Maori students. As a group, national statistics indicate that many underachieve in the education system, with many failing at all levels. Our Maori students' pass rate for both boys and girls was at or above that achieved by our non-Maori students.

PART IV

Putting It All Together

31

Framing

Part of the brain's wiring allows it to make visual meaning from words (Barrett, 1992). If you hear the word "banana," the first thing that happens for most people is that their brain supplies a picture of the fruit or something associated with it.

When we talk to people, we are trying to create a picture that they will understand.

However, sometimes we use words that may create a different message from what we want:

"**Don't** think of a volcano."

"**Don't** think of a volcano with lava pouring down the sides."

"**Don't** think of ash pouring out of the volcano and covering the village below."

"**Don't** think of the villagers running away."

What did you think about? The volcano, right? Thinking about it now, how often do we say things like, "Don't panic" or "Don't forget your homework." It goes even deeper: We may describe an activity or test as difficult before the event has begun or begin by apologizing about the length of time of our lesson and how boring it will be. These comments all sow seeds that may create a negative learning state (Allen, 2001).

Conversely, describing a task as "easy" puts pressure on learners who may then find the task difficult. Imagine what that may do to their self-esteem. It would be better to say, "We are all unique. Some people find certain activities a challenge while others are able to complete them with ease. Remember that your own expectation will shape the result and that practice strengthens your learning."

Research on memory indicates that the words we use about an event will either enhance or detract from the importance that we place on recalling the event in the future (Jensen, 2006). Emotional words literally slow the brain, allowing us a millisecond more time to encode the information. Retailers use the words "sale" and "bargain" to gain this effect (Allen, 2002).

The marketing world knows this well and uses it as a sales technique.
As educators we are salespeople, selling the possibility of learning.

This technique takes practice. To change my bad habits, I began by concentrating on eliminating the word "don't." I would ask one of my colleagues to attend the lesson and to listen specifically for me using the "don't" word. Every time I did, she raised her hand. In the first session, I saw my colleague's hand raise more than twenty times. By the second session, it was down to seven and dropped to two in the third session. Now I monitor it myself, literally clamping my teeth and reshaping the sentence into the positive.

Finally, eliminate the word "try." It is so much more affirming to say "let's do it" rather than "let's try." "Try" has an element of failure already built in. Aim for what you want rather than what you want to avoid.

A frame is there to focus our attention. Let's ensure we focus it on the target.

32

Prewiring

To improve the possibility of achieving the target we can prepare before the event. The brain contains its own major search engine called the reticular activating system (RAS) (Carter, 1998; Howard, 2000). This has the ability to focus our attention nonconsciously.

Have you ever noticed that when you have decided to buy a particular model of car that you keep seeing it in the street? If you read a new word, you are certain to hear it or read it again within the next few weeks; if you are interested in a particular topic, you will pick up a magazine and find an article written on it. The RAS is in operation when we get a phone call from a long lost friend and say, "I was just thinking about you yesterday."

This is the power of focus. As educators, once we are aware of this brain function, we can use it (Allen, 2001, 2002; Smith, 2004):

"There will be a test tomorrow on what we have covered in the topic so far. If you have kept your reviewing schedule up-to-date, this is a great opportunity to show your learning."

Statements such as this give the learner some expectation of what is going to happen in the next learning session. If worded correctly, they not only engender excitement, but also the strong probability of success (Allen, 2002).

It is similar to turning over the garden and digging in the fertilizer weeks before planting.

The number and type of prewiring statements are unlimited. Here are some further examples:

- "If you like excitement, you are going to love the next session."
- "Put up your hand if exploring a new idea is something you like to do. Great, because that is what the next session is about."
- "This home learning will lead right into tomorrow's topic."

- "For about seventy-five percent of you, this next session is probably the most important so far."
- "When you come in tomorrow morning, glance up at the whiteboard, and you will see something that is very important for you to know."

Prewiring frames the mind and creates a state of anticipation. It can be done through oral statements, artwork or posters, metaphors or sayings displayed on the wall, or direct experiences before the unit study begins (DePorter, Reardon, & Singer-Nourie, 1999; Tate, 2004). Here are some specific examples of how to use prewiring:

- You may want to have an area where you stand or display the prewiring for future events. This may be completed at the same time every day; this then becomes an important learning ritual.
- Place a small whiteboard at your door and write on it a daily greeting, reminders, and things to look forward to. Phrases such as, "Remember to enter the room with a smile" are beneficial.
- Use "home learning" time as a prewire, allowing students time to research the next topic before it begins.
- Use spot quizzes followed with comments such as, "Well done. Next week you will be able to get all of these answers correct and many more besides."

Select only important events to prewire. The scarcity factor is important. If something becomes a ritual, it no longer triggers noradrenaline and other "focusing" brain hormones. Rather than excitement, constant exposure creates apathy towards the event and the motivation for learning is reduced.

Let's not wait until tomorrow to make things happen.

33

Loops

Have you ever had the experience of talking to someone and forgetting to tell him something? Then, you find that when he has walked away you suddenly remember what you wanted to say. This is often very frustrating, because it may have been a vital piece of information that would help to make sense of the discussion. What I have just done is to give you an example of using a loop through an example of an unfinished loop (Allen, 2001).

By relating a common situation, I have created a loop back to something that you have probably also personally experienced. At the same time, the actual situation that I used is an example of an unfinished loop because important parts of the conversation were not completed.

The busy teacher in the classroom is asked many questions in a day. Sometimes you may say to the student, "Ask me again later" or "I'll tell you later," and then forget to do so. The learner then goes away thinking that she only asked one question and didn't even get a proper answer. This becomes an unfinished loop.

The brain loves making patterns to create meaning (Dispenza, 2007). The more completed loops that occur in relationship to the learning, the more memory banks are activated, and therefore the higher the chance of accurate recall (Barrett, 1992).

Loops can be

- **short-term,** as in finishing off a statement or answer, or completing a learning frame.
- **mid-term,** as in finishing work that you have begun. papier-maché puppets are often a good example.
- **long-term,** as in linking together work throughout the year as themes.
- **future-focused,** as in the use of prewiring.

Prewiring is a form of unfinished loop that you have purposefully set up to finish at a later date (Allen, 2002). An example of a prewiring statement is,

"Tomorrow we are going to explore a very exciting idea. I'm looking forward to it and I'm sure that you are, too."

USING LOOPS IN THE CLASSROOM

- Sometimes you might find it worthwhile to appoint class "loopers." Their job is to jot down any unfinished business.
- Another thing to do is consciously respond to the person who has a question by saying, "Thank you, I'll finish that loop later. Please remind me at the end of the session if I have not already done so."
- Yet another way is to have an "unfinished business" time at the end of each session to complete any loops with questions and discussion.
- Reintroducing past learning or practicing a known skill, such as times tables, maintains and strengthens existing loops.
- A quiz or test can reveal unfinished or forgotten loops. Give the "why" before the test so that stress levels are lessened. For example, you might say, "We are having this review of our learning to see if we need to strengthen any learning loops."
- As a form of reflection, mind maps or graphic organizers will often reveal incomplete loops to the learner.
- Daily overviews and their relationships to yesterday's learning are important.
- Themes are a constant loop, continually being finished and then reopened with new learning.

A piece of rope is more useful when it is tied to something.

34

Feedback

An important part of the loop is the feedback process. Accurate feedback is vital for learners so that they fully understand the "next step" required in their learning (deBono, 1995; Gelb, 1995; Jensen, 2005, 2006). It begins with the internal chatter before, during, and after the task and is often concerned with how we perceive our ability. "By facilitating students' attentional focus on personal goals and immediate feedback, we can actually help their brains direct their attention by bringing these goals to a conscious level" (Kaufeldt, 2001).

To do this we need a range of focus questions (Harmin, 1998):

- What have I learned?
- What do I now know that I didn't know before?
- What have I learned about myself?
- Where am I performing well and where do I need to improve?

Traditionally, reviews are done in a formal manner such as a test. We now know that to make memories meaningful, we need to add emotion in the form of fun, movement, and the unexpected (Chernow, 1997).

There are many simple reviews that provide emotion to feedback:

- Have students sit in pairs with a piece of string about thirty centimeters long. The first student takes the string, and while winding it around her finger, recalls three new things she learned that day. The second student now has his turn.
- Again sitting in pairs, the first person recalls a fact, and then partners clap hands with each other. Now it is time for the second person to recall a point. See how long the recall/clap cycle can be maintained.
- Form groups of four to eight people. Select someone to begin the review. That person states an important fact and then passes a Koosh® ball or "talking object" in a clockwise direction to the next person in the circle.

- Form a large circle using all class members. Play music and throw three indoor Frisbees® around. When the music stops, each person who is holding a Frisbee® or is closest to a Frisbee® on the floor has to recall certain facts about a topic. To lower stress, I number the Frisbees® and put a corresponding number and question on the whiteboard, e.g., "(1) Spell a word on your list. (2) Tell something that you have learned about bees in science this week. (3) Explain what a comma, semi-colon, or exclamation point is used for in a sentence." Stress levels can be further lowered by allowing the partner on either side to help.
- Use a large die for a similar review. This time, write six questions on the board, one for each side of the die. Siting in groups of six to eight, students take turns throwing the die. Each person answers the question that corresponds to the number thrown.
- Have students sit in pairs. The partners takes turns holding up three fingers and touching them one at a time as they recall three important details on a topic.
- Sitting in pairs again, one person is the expert and the other the interviewer. In a given time frame, the interviewer asks a series of questions about the topic while the expert answers.
- Make a simple mind map of the day's learning.
- Use graphic organizers as a review to show relationships.
- Do the same with a flowchart to recall sequence.
- Have a fun true/false quiz in which participants move to answer. If they think the answer is true, they move to one side of the room; if false, they move to the other side of the room; if they are unsure, they do not move.
- Make a statement and then ask students to stand in a continuum, with those who strongly agree at one end and those who strongly disagree at the other.
- Have learners complete these statements on either side of a small card: Side A—"I know that _____. Side B—"I still have a question about _____." Students circulate throughout the group in order to find answers for their questions, as well as help others to answer theirs.
- Use flashcards that recall key points of a topic. This can be done in teams to add competitive emotions, which strengthen memory.
- Have students use a rubric assessment frame to either self-reflect or reflect with the teacher. This will provide vital feedback for your next learning goals.
- Most party games can be easily converted into reviews. For example, "spin the bottle" can be used to select reviewers, as can the simple activity of tossing a coin.

By acknowledging what we have learned, we give meaning to life.

This is a review song that I wrote to assist a class of six- to seven-year-olds who were having difficulty remembering how to correctly remember the essential steps involved when writing a letter. They sang it in a large, outside space with the teacher in the role of "drill sergeant." As the teacher chanted the first line, the students chorused back and began to march. Movement, rhythm, and the catchy tune worked. The teacher noticed that back in class, many students could be heard quietly singing the song as their letters took shape, this time in the correct order.

We're good at writing letters now.

We're good at writing letters now.

Let us show you, we know how.

Let us show you, we know how.

Put the address then leave a space.

Put the address then leave a space.

Now comes the date in the next place.

Now comes the date in the next place.

Drop a line, "Dear Whatshisname."

Drop a line, "Dear Whatshisname."

All letters, they begin the same.

All letters, they begin the same.

Now write the letter to your friend.

Now write the letter to your friend.

Move down a line, it is the end.

Move down a line, it is the end.

Sign it!

Sign it

Seal it!

Seal it!

Stamp it!

Stamp it!

Post it!

Post it!

We're good at writing letters now.

We're good at writing letters now.

Let us tell you, we know how.

Let us tell you, we know how.

Mind Maps and Mindscapes

Tony Buzan (1997) invented the concept of mind mapping after studying the structures that nature uses in the brain, seeds, cells, and plants. Mind mapping is both sequential and random; visual in that it involves words, symbols, and color; and extremely flexible in the way it can be designed and used (Gelb, 1995).

Mindscapes are a larger version that can be created using a wall with teams contributing their ideas at the same time (Marguiles, 1992). Mind maps and mindscapes are a great way to review, because they have something in them that appeals to most learners (Buzan, 1997).

There are some basic rules to follow so that the mind-mapping processes can be developed (Gelb, 1995; Marguiles, 1992):

- **Turn your piece of paper to "landscape."** Generally our reading processes are left-to-right, rather than vertical; turning the paper provides more space for our ideas to flow.
- **Use a central image to conceptualize the mind-mapping topic**. This should be one key word or image and needs to involve at least three appropriate colors as a memory stimulant.
- **The main ideas grow from the central image** like branches extending from the trunk of a tree.
- **Print in block letters**. This is clearest medium for the eye/brain connection.
- **Mind maps are similar to speed-reading:** They both rely on the use of key words to convey meaning. Each main branch only needs one or two key words to trigger the memory.
- **To indicate completion of the idea**, make your written words the same length as the lines they sit on.
- **Radiate "twigs" with sub-ideas** from the main branches.

- **Vary the size of the words** to denote importance.
- **Use codes, pictures, symbols, and arrows** to shows links.
- **There is no correct starting position once the central image has been established**. Many people prefer to begin at the "one o'clock" point, but this is an individual choice.
- **It is not necessary to work in sequential order**. If you are working on one concept branch of the mind map and you remember a point from a separate concept, write it on its own branch while you still remember. This is an advantage over traditional notes that generally require you to work in order.
- **Some people associate each arm with a separate color.** Others use color randomly. It is an individual choice.

We began by teaching five-year-olds the mind-mapping process. Because they were so young and this was a new experience, it was important to connect with what they already knew.

The class had been studying how birds nested in trees, so it was useful to refer to the central picture as a log with branches coming out. The words were to be written on the branches leading outwards from the trunk. However, even with this imagery, sometimes mistakes still occurred.

Five-year-olds, as kindergarten teachers know, will literally do as you say. Because I instructed them to begin their word at the trunk and move outwards, this is what they did. This was fine on the right-hand side of the page; however, on the left-side of the page, they wrote backwards! Good listening skills, but not what I intended.

Be warned. Students have the marvelous ability to keep you grounded.

Note that some students find it difficult to take initial notes in an elaborate mind map. It is very acceptable to take full notes and then transfer them as a memory prompt.

Connect your thoughts. Connect your world.

36

Reflection

Our nonstop world, built on instant gratification, has a lot to answer for. Rather than savoring the process and the moment, much of life can be spent ticking off achievement lists. As one teacher was heard to say, "I managed to cover the whole curriculum this year. Unfortunately, only some of the children came with me."

Reflection is such a vital part of the learning process (Canfield, 2005; deBono, 1994; Kraus, 2002; Udall & Daniels, 1991). If we do not spend time reflecting, then why did we bother with the learning?

The reflection process has four main components (Scaddan, 2002):

Restate the learning goal:
- What did we hope to achieve?
- What was the purpose?

Review the process:
- What did we actually do?
- What did we achieve?
- What process and steps did we follow?

Provide feedback about what we learned:
- What did I learn?
- What new skills have I developed?

Reflect on what has transferred:
- Where does this sit in my portfolio of life skills?
- How has my thinking or attitudes changed?
- How can I use it in real life?

The application to real life is what gives learning its ultimate meaning (Kovalik, 1997). Learning can be a fun, innovative, or emotional experience; if it does not have a clear use, however, the brain deletes it.

With the emphasis on covering the crowded curriculum, too often something is taught once, and then we feel that we need to move on to the next step. The essence, the reflection, and the real-life usage are ignored.

Reflection doesn't just happen. It needs to be taught, and this can be done in many ways (deBono, 1995):

- Because many students are so strongly visual and kinesthetic, mind maps often prove to be a real asset for this task. Here we can go through the complete process of what we were expected to learn, what steps we followed, what we actually learned, and how we will use it.
- In pairs, have students discuss three things they learned that day.
- Have students use learning diaries to reflect. This has the added advantage that previous weeks can be referred back to in order to check progress.
- Reflection may be done as a whole class, especially regarding behavioral or emotional intelligence issues. The process is enhanced when the real-life usage is identified. For younger learners, the teacher may be required to provide this. As students become more mature, they should add their own thoughts.
- The next stage is for the teacher to ask, "Who can see how we can use what we have learned to solve this problem?" Now we have higher-level thinking in action, rather than the teacher doing all the work.
- Use the term "reflection" with students so they develop a full understanding.
- Nonfiction articles are a great resource to practice the technique with questions such as, "What do you think the person learned from this event?"

At the beginning, students may find reflection challenging because it is a new skill. Persevere with the process—it is a vital part of the learning loop.

*If we continue to spoon-feed students, the only thing they will
recognize is the shape of the spoon.*

37

Lo, Mo, and Ho Questions

Part of the reflection process is the development of questioning techniques (Costa, 2000). "It is more important for students to learn what questions to ask—and how to ask them—than to learn the answers" (Sternberg & Grigorenko, 2000).

Effective questioning is highly skilled. Research indicates that many of the questions we ask lack focus, depth, and purpose (Allen, 2002; Frangenheim, 1998; Udall, 1997).

The average teacher asks up to four hundred questions a day, with up to ten being asked in a minute (Fogarty, 2002; Katterns, 2002)! As few as twenty of these questions actually require answers that promote higher-level thinking. For the other 380 questions,

- the teacher often doesn't require an answer: "Do you really think that I want to see this?"
- the teacher gives the answer: "What type of tree do you think this is? Anyone? Anyone? No, then it is a pine tree. I thought you would know that."
- the teacher moves rapidly on to another person to answer.

Then there is the form of the question. Many are ambiguous or repeatedly extended to so that the expected answer becomes more and more obscure (Allen, 2002; Fogarty, 2002):

"Do you think that we would find this object inside or outside? Maybe it could be found in both, but which one is more likely? If it was inside or outside, and I'm not saying which or giving you a hint, where would we find it in these places? Please be specific."

105

Then there is the type of question. In an average classroom, an astounding eighty percent of questions are lower-order (Lo) questions (Katterns, 2002). Here are some examples of types of lower-order questions:

- simple recall
- yes/no
- definitions
- observe and describe
- observe and identify
- designate

These questions have their place but are not designed to stimulate higher-level thinking. When you plan your work, aim to move students higher in the thinking process. Include a range of questions in the middle- and higher-order range (Mo and Ho).

Middle-order involves understanding and detecting and includes questions that ask learners to do these things:

- explain their ideas and feelings
- interpret, define in their own words, illustrate, and paraphrase
- relate, classify, associate, and discriminate
- combine
- summarize
- generalize
- compare and contrast
- analyze

Higher-order questions are inventing and evaluating:

- predict, hypothesize, or speculate
- apply or transfer
- infer, estimate, conclude
- create
- judge
- value
- defend or argue against
- justify choice

Students will not find the process of answering higher- and middle-order questions easy, and teachers often struggle with asking them. It will require teachers to develop sequential skill growth. I recommend that you take these steps:

- Practice your questioning techniques, and you will find that they rapidly improve.
- At least in the early stages, write questions down in your planning. Once you became more expert, this will no longer be necessary.

- Watch a video of yourself asking questions; it will provide you with valuable feedback.

Remember that it is short-term pain for long-term gain. The old methods of questioning are a lot easier, but in relying on them, we deprive the students of an opportunity to learn.

The brain learns by constantly questioning.

38

Inclusive Responses

To improve both questioning and answering, it is important to create the right climate. Unfortunately, students soon learn that there is an (unintended) ranking system operating in many classrooms. This is generated in two ways: by the teacher choosing only certain people to answer and by the teacher's responses to their answers.

Responses to students' answers often include clues about how the teacher is ranking students:

- "Mmmm."
- "OK . . . ."
- "Excellent. Thank you, John."
- "Do you really think that or weren't you listening?"

As the teacher moves around the room, this rating system is recorded in students' minds in conscious and nonconscious ways (Allen, 2002).

Nobody wants a negative ranking, so the easy answer is . . . don't answer.

As a result, the average classroom becomes a place where three to five students do the majority of the responding (Fogarty, 2002; Rief & Heimburge, 1996). Not only that, when the correct response is given, the questioning process finishes.

"Excellent, John. You are completely correct. Well done." The teacher then moves on to the next part of the lesson.

Students soon learn that if they wait long enough, somebody will provide the correct answer, and they can continue to sit in an uninvolved state.

This game is repeated day after day. From a classroom management point of view, it is quick and safe, but it does not encourage learning (Allen, 2002). To remedy this situation, we need to move from rating the answer and finishing the process as soon as a correct response is given to encouraging participation.

Instead, practice the art of inclusive responses. Ask a question and respond to answers with a range of comments that acknowledge effort and participation:

- "Good effort."
- "Thank you."
- "Thanks. Anyone else?"
- "I appreciate your contribution."
- "Thanks for sharing your ideas."
- "Thanks for taking part."
- "Great participation."

In this process it is important to acknowledge the response, but avoid rating the answer in any form. If the correct answer is supplied, the acknowledgement is still made regarding the participation, and the process continues. This encourages students to think through a wider range of possibilities, which encourages higher-level processing.

This process should continue for up to two minutes. If the correct response is given, acknowledge it with an inclusive statement and move on. Remember, we are seeking participation; your tone of voice, facial expression, and body language will either encourage or discourage the process.

It is important that the correct answer is revealed within two minutes so that memory is accurate. This is part of the inclusive process. The students who gave correct answers know who they are, but we do not need to acknowledge them individually, as this can emphasize the class ranking system. Instead we respond with, "The correct answer was pine trees, and we did hear that. Thank you, everyone, for taking part."

How long do we continue this practice? Until all learners are happy to participate and understand that there is an obligation to do so (Allen, 2002; Fogarty, 2002; Rief & Heimburge, 1996).

Many students spend their school life "camouflaged" so they can hide from the stress of responding.

"He doesn't tell us if we're right."

I was working once again in our "Learn to Learn" program with senior students and we were practicing how to reference material when completing an assignment. During this particular lesson, I was at times using inclusive statements so that the students would begin to think on a deeper level.

Initially, this proved to be an uncomfortable process for them, and there were a variety of reactions. One of the senior girls answered a question to which I replied, "Thanks very much. Does anyone else have an answer?"

(Continued)

(Continued)

I looked back at her a short time later and overheard her saying to one of her friends, "He doesn't even tell us if we're right or wrong." Suddenly her eyes lit up. "I know what you're doing," she said. "You don't care if we are right. You just want us to think for ourselves!"

Such a simple truth had a profound effect on her. She changed from being a nonengaged student to one who relished participation, putting forward a range of ideas and presenting arguments to justify them.

This slowly grew until a larger group began to follow her lead. The other students began to see the excitement of putting forward an idea and learning that there is generally more than one correct answer and that the exploration and testing of possibilities was what learning was all about. Of course not all students took this on board, however over the next few weeks more and more of the class began to think rather than to sit waiting for information to come their way.

SOURCE: Michael A. Scaddan

39

Response Time

Questioning is an art. One of the often-overlooked skills is allowing time for response. For the typical teacher, the response time to a question is as little as one second, whether the classroom was in the United States (Fogarty, 2002) or New Zealand (Katterns, 2002)!

After this brief time, teachers either move on to another student or answer the question themselves. Again, the unwritten rule of the classroom is highlighted for students: If I just sit here with a puzzled look on my face, the teacher will soon move on.

The second thing that happens with response time is that when teachers do try to increase the wait time, the silence often becomes awkward, and so they rephrase or repeat the question. All that this does is complicate the issue (Katterns, 2002).

Here is an example from a history lesson:

History teacher: "What was the cause of the first world war?" No response.

History teacher: "What I mean is, which countries were involved and what was the role of the various treaties and how were these affected by the death of a little-known duke?" Silence, followed by a tentative reply.

Student: "Germany?"

History teacher: "No. You obviously didn't listen to the question."

No wonder the students were confused. Instead of one simple question, they now had a confusion of information to the point where they were unsure of not only what to respond to, but also how to respond. Does the question require an in-depth answer, a simple yes or no, or should they wait for clarification?

TO ENCOURAGE A HIGHER DEGREE OF LEARNING

- **First, only ask questions that students will have a fair chance of answering.** Even when they are asked to predict, they should have a foundation of prior information to work with. Bloom's Taxonomy can be of great assistance here (Bloom, 1956).
- **Avoid giving clues.** We all process in unique ways. I'm sure that you have taken part in a board game where "helpful hints" only confuse the issue. Instead, you may allow time for students to discuss the question with a partner to explore possibilities or encourage them to ask questions of you in order to gain more information.
- **Instead of rephrasing or repeating the question, ask students a question and then deliberately sit and wait for a response.** The minutes will seem to drag, but in fact it won't be that long. If there is no response after thirty seconds or so, say, "That's fine. I'll come back to that question again in another few minutes," and then do so.
- **At times, structure a finite time for processing.** Ask the question and then let them know that they have two minutes to think of an answer. They may want to work individually or in pairs. Have the question written on the board so that visual learners can refer back to it, thus avoiding the response, "What was the question again?"
- **Try sitting in a circle at question time so it is more inclusive.** To lessen the emphasis on you, ask the question standing up or sitting up straight and then deliberately slip down to become part of the scenery while responses are forthcoming.
- **The inability to respond is normal.** If a student has her hand up and when chosen cannot remember her answer, it is a typical reaction to perceived stress, or it may be that the answer has dropped out of the immediate memory's fifteen- to twenty-second time span.
- **Accept the answer as genuine.** If you respond with, "What I think you are trying to say is . . ." you are not only presuming that your response is better, but you are now doing the higher-level thinking for them.
- **Allow time for correction.** When students feel that they can change their answers without penalty, the class learning culture is operating well.
- **Remember not to accept the first correct response.** This is when the inclusive statement routine works extremely well (Allen, 2002).
- **Provide a clear "why" for the process.** Explain that you are asking questions this way because "it is the brain that does the work that does the learning," and your job is to help them to learn.
- **Changing a habit can be challenging.** Remember, as with any new skill, this may be uncomfortable to begin with, but it is well worth the effort!

A genuine moment given freely is invaluable.

40

Hands-Free

An Obligation to Answer

As your students get used to the different styles of questions and response techniques, you can introduce an additional concept. This is the obligation to answer even if your hand is not raised (Raffini, 1996).

As part of "The Game of School and How to Play It," we teach that a non-response, blank stare, or a shrug of the shoulders is not the best body language to use if you want to make a positive impression (Scaddan, 2002). As teachers, we also know that in many classes, only five or six students regularly raise their hands while the majority opts out (Allen, 2002; Rief & Heimburge, 1996).

Delay the introduction of this obligation until you have built a positive culture. It is important to make sure that the process is not too stressful, but it is also important to have an expectation that students will take a leading role in their learning (deBono, 1995).

WAYS TO GO HANDS-FREE

- This can be introduced even with young students by having students gather in a group. Explain that you will ask a question, and after a signal is given (e.g., blowing a train whistle), you will choose people to answer. Their hands must remain behind their backs. Of course, they are so enthusiastic that you may need to make it into a game to see who can keep their answer to themselves until chosen.
- This is an opportunity to use the inclusive responses mentioned in Tool 38, thanking students for their contribution rather than the accuracy of the answer.

113

- To ease the tension and to counter anyone calling out, I might ask the question and then say, "When I blow the whistle, I want you all to call out an answer." At other times, after calling on a few students and getting the same answer, I ask "Who else knew that?" Then even the ones who didn't can enjoy the celebration.

- From Grade 5 and beyond, it is beneficial to always begin with the "why," explaining that all of us have had the experience where we didn't give an answer for various reasons and then another student gave that answer and received lots of praise. I then ask a question and call a student's name. The student either responds with an answer or is expected to say, "I'm not sure." If the latter, my response is "Fine, I'll get back to you." I then must remember to do this so that the loop is complete. If the response is still "I'm not sure," I might ask the student to check his or her notes and if the answer is not there, to write it down.

- Ask a question with a yes or no response and have students move to a designated side of the room to indicate their choices.

- Ask a question and give three possible answers. Make sure that the answers are varied. If they are too similar, it can be designed confusion.

- Have each student write an answer to that question and share it with at least three other people. Review responses and then share the correct answer. If any of the students had wrong answers, ensure that they note the correct one. Some people may say that this is cheating; I view it is a shared educational opportunity in which learners are exposed to the correct answer by communication with their peers.

- Ask a question and, in a given time frame, students must identify and stand with a partner who has the same answer. Play a short piece of music to help measure the time and to increase emotion.

- Pin up a series of questions in different parts of the room and then have teams of two students move around answering them. This can be designed like a car rally, where answers need to be recorded in the correct sequence to complete a message—if you wish to add a competitive edge.

Whichever methods are used, it is vital that we change the culture and involve all students in the process of learning.

Involvement in learning is a vital memory process.

During a shared reading session, I told the students that we would be having a "hands-free" questioning session. We often informed them in advance so they knew what to expect. During the reading, both the students and I were asking questions and asking for responses. I observed the students using my strategies when they said, "That's OK, but I'll get back to you" or "Just think about that, and I'll ask you soon" when a student was asked who was not sure of the answer.

All the students who were called upon were confident to reply, and if they didn't know the answer, they were given the opportunity to find out as a follow-up. It was a very productive lesson with a sense of achievement felt by all.

SOURCE: Shannon Robinson, elementary teacher in New Zealand and England

Conclusion

Reviews are very important
'cause they make you think.
Da Do Ron Ron Ron
Da Do Ron Ron
If you don't know the answer,
you have missed the link.
Da Do Ron Ron Ron
Da Do Ron Ron
They make memory stick.
Keep our neurons slick.
Give us the answers quick.
Da Do Ron Ron Ron
Da Do Ron Ron
If your memory doesn't work,
it can be a concern.
Da Do Ron Ron Ron
Da Do Ron Ron
Reviews are very important
'cause they help you learn.
Da Do Ron Ron Ron
Da Do Ron Ron
Do them lots of times—
activities or make up rhymes.
10, 24, 7*
Da Do Ron Ron Ron
Da Do Ron Ron

---

*To aid memory retention, review after ten minutes, twenty four hours, and seven days.

I hope that you kept a journal of your successes, modifications, and mistakes. Many of us still teach on an intuitive level, and that means that we cannot pass on our knowledge to others.

Sir Laurence Olivier came off the stage once after a memorable performance. A fellow actor found him in tears and asked, "Why are you crying? That was a magnificent performance."

"I know," said Sir Laurence. "The problem is I don't know how to do it again."

BRAIN-BASED REVIEW

1. Take time to reflect on the process of teaching and how you have incorporated the tools into your program.

2. What resources have you been able to develop so far, including strategies, material, and personal development?

3. What resources do you need to build up?

4. What are your itches—the areas of challenge that still need to be "scratched"?

5. Are there any books that you now need to read?

6. What else would you like learning tools about? Please e-mail me if you have suggestions.

7. Where do you go from here? It is very important to keep the development process going. Your brain will now be attuned to this process and will help you find the way.

Think about teaching these processes to others, as this will reinforce what you know and clarify issues that are still "rough draft."

In this modern era, there is a high expectation on teachers to achieve results, cover the curriculum, and achieve a high pass rate in varying forms of assessment. As a result, the teacher is often doing more and more of the work because that appears to be more efficient.

Students may pass the assessment, but have they learned anything or are the answers just something to forget five minutes after the test?

Brain-compatible learning involves students to a high degree in the learning process so that they are intrinsically motivated to succeed. This book has been written to provide you with a structure to develop the process. Remember to "do less and do it better," both in your teaching and during this change process.

If I can assist you or your school with the development of brain-compatible learning, "Learn to Learn" programs, "The Game of School and How to Play It," or any other aspect of professional development, please contact me at the e-mail address listed in About the Author in the front of the book.

Enjoy the journey.

Suggested Reading

Barrett, S. (1992). *It's all in your head . . . .* Minneapolis, MN: Free Spirit.

Benzwie, T. (1998). *A moving experience.* Tucson, AZ: Zephyr Press.

Buzan, T. (1997). *Use your memory.* London: BBC Books.

Caine, G., & Caine, R. (1994). *Making connections.* Menlo Park, CA: Addison-Wesley.

Caine, G., & Caine, R. (1997). *Unleashing the power of perceptual change.* Alexandria, VA: Association for Supervision and Curriculum Development.

Caine, G., Caine, R., & Crowell, S. (1999). *Mind shifts.* Tucson, AZ: Zephyr Press.

Campbell, D. (1992). *Introduction to the musical brain.* St. Louis, MO: MMB Music.

Cohen, D. (1996). *The secret language of the mind.* London: Duncan Baird.

Costa, A. (1991). *The school as a home for the mind.* Heatherton, Australia: Hawker Brownlow Education.

Costa, A., & Kallick, B. (2000). *Activating and engaging habits of mind.* Alexandria, VA: Association for Supervision and Curriculum Development.

Costa, A., & Kallick, B. (2000). *Assessing and reporting on habits of mind.* Alexandria, VA: Association for Supervision and Curriculum Development.

Costa, A., & Kallick, B. (2000). *Integrating and sustaining habits of mind.* Alexandra, VA: Association for Supervision and Curriculum Development.

Covey, Stephen. (1997). *The 7 habits of highly effective people.* Melbourne, Australia: The Business Library.

Dennison, P., & Dennison, G. (1994). *Brain gym.* Ventura, CA: Edu-Kinesthetics.

Editors of *Scientific American.* (1999). *The Scientific American book of the brain.* Gulford, CT: Lyons Press.

Glasser, N. (Ed). (1989). *Control theory in the practice of reality therapy.* New York: Harper & Row.

Glasser, W., & Glasser, C. (1998*). Choice: The flip side of control.* Chatsworth, CA: The William Glasser Institute.

Greenfield, S. (1997). *The human brain.* New York: Basic Books.

Gregory, R. (1987). *The Oxford companion to the mind.* Oxford: Oxford University Press.

Healy, J. (1999). *Failure to connect.* New York: Touchstone.

Horgan, J. (1999). *The undiscovered mind.* London: Weidenfeld & Nicholson.

Jensen, E. (1988). *Map your way to better grades.* Los Angeles: Learning Forum.

Jensen, E. (1989). *Student success secrets.* New York: Barron's Educational Series.

Jensen, E. (1995). *Brain-based learning and teaching.* Del Mar, CA: Turning Point.

Jensen, E. (1995) *Super teaching.* Del Mar, CA: Turning Point.

Jensen, E. (1995). *The learning brain.* Del Mar, CA: Turning Point.

Jensen, E. (1997). *Brain-compatible strategies.* Del Mar, CA: Turning Point.

Jensen, E. (1997). *Bright brain.* Del Mar, CA: Turning Point.

Jensen, E. (1997). *B's and A's in 30 days.* New York: Barron's Educational Series.

Jensen, E. (1997). *Completing the puzzle.* San Diego, CA: The Brain Store.

Jensen, E. (1998). *Super mapping* [video]. San Diego, CA: The Brain Store.

Jensen, E. (2000). *Learning with the body in mind.* San Diego, CA: The Brain Store.

Jensen, E. (2000). *Music with the brain in mind.* San Diego, CA: The Brain Store.

Jensen, E. (2003). *Tools for engagement.* San Diego, CA: The Brain Store.

Jensen, E. (2005). *Teaching with the brain in mind* (2nd ed.). Alexandria, VA: Association for Supervision and Curriculum Development.

Jensen, E., & Dabney, M. (2000). *Learning smarter.* San Diego: The Brain Store.

Juan, S. (2000). *The odd brain.* Sydney, Australia: Harper Collins.

Karges-Bone, L. (1996). *Beyond hands-on.* Carthage, IL: Teaching & Learning.

Keith, K. (2001). *The paradoxical commandments.* Sydney, Australia: Hodder.

McWilliams, P. (1994). *Life 101.* Los Angeles: Prelude Press.

Oliver, C., & Bowler, R. (1996). *Learning to learn.* New York: Simon & Schuster.

Prashnig, B. (1996). *Diversity is our strength.* Auckland, New Zealand: Profile Books.

Prashnig, B. (1998). *The power of diversity.* Auckland, New Zealand: David Bateman.

Raffini, J. (1996). *150 ways to increase intrinsic motivation in the classroom.* Boston: Allyn & Bacon.

Rief, S., & Heimburge, J. (1996). *How to reach and teach all children in the inclusive classroom.* New York: The Center for Applied Research in Education.

Robbins A. (1992). *Awaken the giant within.* New York: Fireside.

Rose, C., & Nicholl, M. (1997). *Accelerated learning for the 21st century.* New York: Piatkus.

Rupp, R. (1998). *Committed to memory.* London: Aurum Press.

Sapolsky, R. (1998). *Why zebras don't get ulcers.* New York: W. H. Freeman.

Scaddan, M. (Producer). (2002). *The hairy brain school* [video]. Tauranga, New Zealand: Te Puna School.

Scaddan, M. (Producer). (2003). *Reviews from the hairy brain school* [video]. Tauranga, New Zealand: Te Puna School.

Scaddan, M. (2002). *Twenty rules of the game of school.* Tauranga, New Zealand: Brain Stems.

Siegel, D. (1999). *The developing mind.* New York: Guilford Press.

Smith, A. (2004). *The brain's behind it.* Stafford, United Kingdom: Network Educational Press.

Smith, A., Lovatt, M., & Wise, D. (2003). *Accelerated learning: A user's guide.* Stafford, United Kingdom: Network Educational Press.

Sousa, D. (1998). *Learning manual for how the brain learns.* Thousand Oaks, CA: Corwin Press.

Sousa, D. (2006). *How the brain learns* (3rd ed.). Thousand Oaks, CA: Corwin Press.

Sousa, D. (2007). *How the special needs brain works* (2nd ed.). Thousand Oaks, CA: Corwin Press.

Sprenger, M. (2002). *Becoming a "wiz" at brain-based teaching.* Thousand Oaks, CA: Corwin Press.

Sternberg, R., & Grigorenko, E. (2008). *Teaching for successful intelligence* (2nd ed.). Thousand Oaks, CA: Corwin Press.

Stine, J. M. (1997). *Double your brain power.* Paramus, NJ: Prentice Hall.

Sylwester, R. (2000). *A biological brain in a cultural classroom.* Thousand Oaks, CA: Corwin Press.

Tate, M. (2004). *"Sit and get" won't grow dendrites.* Thousand Oaks, CA: Corwin Press.

Tate, M. (2007). *Shouting won't grow dendrites.* Thousand Oaks, CA: Corwin Press.

Teacher Created Resources. (1999). *Multiple intelligences activities.* Westminster, CA: Author.

The New City School. (1994). *Celebrating multiple intelligences: Teaching for success.* St. Louis, MO: Faculty of the New City School.

The New City School. (1996). *Succeeding with multiple intelligences: Teaching through the personal intelligences.* St Louis, MO: Faculty of the New City School.

Torrance, E. P., & Sisk, D. (2001). *Gifted and talented children in the regular classroom.* Buffalo, NY: Creative Education Foundation Press.

Tubesing, N. (1997). *Instant icebreakers.* Duluth, MN: Whole Person Associates.

Udall, A. (1997). *Big questions, big ideas.* Tucson, AZ: Zephyr Press.

Udall, A., & Daniels, J. (1991). *Creating the thoughtful classroom.* Tucson, AZ: Zephyr Press.

Wilson, P. (1995). *Instant calm.* Ringwood, Australia: Penguin.

Winter, A., & Winter, R. (1997). *Brain workout.* New York: St. Martins Press.

Wolfe, P. (2001). *Brain matters: Translating research into classroom practice.* Alexandria, VA: Association for Supervision and Curriculum Development.

Zukav, G. (2000). *Soul stories.* New York: Fireside.

References

Tool 1. Emotional Links

Borba, M. (2001). *Building moral intelligence.* San Francisco: Jossey-Bass.

Carter, R. (1998). *Mapping the mind.* London: Weidenfield & Nicholson.

DePorter, B., Reardon, M., & Singer-Nourie, S. (1999). *Quantum teaching.* Boston: Allyn & Bacon.

Goleman, D. (1996). *Emotional intelligence.* London: Bloomsbury.

Jensen, E. (2005). *Teaching with the brain in mind* (2nd ed.). Alexandra, VA: Association for Supervision and Curriculum Development.

LeDoux, J. (1996). *The emotional brain.* New York: Simon & Schuster.

Prentice, C. (2007). *When people matter most.* Wellington, New Zealand: Dunmore.

Tool 2. Metaphors

Canfield, J., & Hansen, M. V. (2003). *Chicken soup for the soul: Living your dreams.* Deerfield Beach, FL: Health Communications.

Carr, T. (1998). *Monday morning messages.* Chapin, SC: Youthlight.

Gelb, M. (1995). *Thinking for a change.* London: Aurum Press.

Levin, F. (2003). *Mapping the mind.* London: Karnac Books.

Owen, N. (2001). *The magic of metaphor.* Bancyfelin, United Kingdom: Crown House.

Sharma, R. (2006). *The greatness guide.* London: Harper Element.

Tate, M. (2004). *"Sit and get" won't grow dendrites.* Thousand Oaks, CA: Corwin Press.

Tool 3. Rules, Guidelines, and Agreements

Gibbs, J. (1995). *Tribes.* Sausalito CA: Center Source.

Glasser, W. (1992). *The quality school.* New York: Harper Collins.

Glasser, W. (1998). *Choice theory.* New York: Harper Perennial.

Kaufeldt, M. (2001). *Begin with the brain.* Thousand Oaks, CA: Corwin Press.

Kohn, A. (1996). *Beyond discipline: From compliance to community.* Alexandra, VA: Association for Supervision and Curriculum Development.

Rief, S., & Heimburge, J. (1996). *How to reach & teach all children in the inclusive classroom.* New York: The Center for Applied Research in Education.

Tool 4. Choice

Dennet, D. (1996). *Kinds of minds.* London: Science Masters.

DePorter, B., Reardon, M., & Singer-Nourie, S. (1999). *Quantum teaching.* Boston: Allyn & Bacon.

Fogarty, R. (2002). *Brain compatible classrooms.* Thousand Oaks, CA: Corwin Press.

Glasser, W. (1998). *Choice theory.* New York: Harper Perennial.

Howard, P. (2000). *The owner's manual for the brain* (2nd ed.). Atlanta, GA: Bard Press.

Jensen, E. (2006). *Enriching the brain.* San Francisco: Jossey-Bass.

Kovalik, S. (1997). *ITI: The model. Integrated thematic education.* Kent, WA: Susan Kovalik and Associates.

Kraus, S. (2002). *Psychological foundations of success.* San Francisco: Change Planet Press.

Robertson, I. (1999). *Mind sculpture.* London: Bantam Press.

Tool 5. Stress Reduction

Barr, S. (1997). *Tapestries: Exploring identity and culture in the classroom.* Tucson, AZ: Zephyr Press.

Carter, R. (1998). *Mapping the mind.* London: Weidenfield & Nicholson.

Dispenza, J. (2007). *Evolve your brain.* Deerfield Beach, FL: Health Communications.

Howard, P. (2000). *The owner's manual for the brain* (2nd ed.). Atlanta, GA: Bard Press.

Jensen, E. (2006). *Enriching the brain.* San Francisco: Jossey-Bass.

Kotulak, R. (1997). *Inside the brain.* Kansas City, MO: Andrews McMeel.

Sapolsky, R. (1998). *Why zebras don't get ulcers.* New York: W. H. Freeman.

Tool 6. Put-Ups

Carter, R. (2002). *Consciousness.* London: Weidenfield & Nicholson.

Johansen, J., & Hay, L. (1996). *Mind your mind.* Oakleigh, Australia: ASG.

Kehoe, J. (1999). *Mind power into the 21st century.* Vancouver, Canada: Zoetic.

Kotulak, R. (1997). *Inside the brain.* Kansas City, MO: Andrews McMeel.

Murphy, J. (1997). *The power of your subconscious mind.* Sydney, Australia: Simon & Schuster.

Parker, J. (1993). *Build a winning self-image.* Vancouver, Canada: Gateway Research Institute.

Politano, C., & Paquin, J. (2000). *Brain-based learning with class.* Winnipeg, Canada: Portage & Main Press.

Robbins, A. (1991). *Awaken the giant within.* New York: Fireside.

Tool 7. Breathing Techniques

Cameron-Hill, P., & Yates, S. (2000). *You won't die laughing.* Windsor, Australia: Argyle.

Gelb, M. (1995). *Thinking for a change.* London: Aurum Press.

Glazener, L. (2004). *Sensorcises.* Thousand Oaks, CA: Corwin Press.

Joseph, J. (2002). *Brainy parents, brainy kids.* Flagstaff Hill, Australia: Focus Education Australia.

Sapolsky, R. (1998). *Why zebras don't get ulcers.* New York: W. H. Freeman.

Wilson, P. (1995). *Instant calm.* Ringwood, Australia: Penguin Books.

Tool 8. Relaxation

Allica, G. (1990). *Meditation workbook.* Melbourne, Australia: David Lovell.

Cameron-Hill, P., & Yates, S. (2000). *You won't die laughing.* Windsor, Australia: Argyle.

Campbell, D. (1992). *100 ways to improve teaching using your voice & music.* Tucson, AZ: Zephyr Press.

Diamond, M., & Hopson, J. (1998). *Magic trees of the mind.* New York: Penguin.

Glazener, L. (2004) *Sensorcises.* Thousand Oaks, CA: Corwin Press.

Howard, P. (2000). *The owner's manual for the brain* (2nd ed.). Atlanta, GA: Bard Press.

Miles, E. (1997). *Tune your brain.* New York: Berkley.

Sapolsky, R. (1998). *Why zebras don't get ulcers.* New York: W. H. Freeman.

Silberg, J. (1999). *Brain games for babies.* Beltsville, MD: Gryphon House.

Tool 9. Eliminating Extrinsic Rewards

Glasser, W. (1992). *The quality school.* New York: Harper Collins.

Glasser, W. (1993). *The quality school teacher.* New York: Harper Collins.

Kohn, A. (1993). *Punished by rewards.* New York: Houghton Mifflin.

Kohn, A. (1996). *Beyond discipline: From compliance to community.* Alexandra, VA: Association for Supervision and Curriculum Development.

Tool 10. Punishment and Consequences

Biddulph, S., & Biddulph, S. (1998). *More secrets of happy children.* New York: Harper Collins.

Faber, A., & Mazlish, E. (1996). *How to talk so kids can learn.* New York: Fireside.

Gordon, T. (1997). *Family effectiveness training.* Solana Beach, CA: Gordon Training International.

Gottman, J., & Declaire, J. (1997). *The heart of parenting: How to raise an emotionally intelligent child.*

Joseph, J. (2002). *Brainy parents, brainy kids.* Flagstaff Hill, Australia: Focus Education Australia.

Sapolsky, R. (1998). *Why zebras don't get ulcers.* W H Freeman and Company. USA.

Tool 11. Contamination

DePorter, B., Reardon, M., & Singer-Nourie, S. (1999). *Quantum teaching.* Boston: Allyn & Bacon.

Dispenza, J. (2007). *Evolve your brain.* Deerfield Beach, FL: Health Communications.

Howard, P. (2000). *The owner's manual for the brain* (2nd ed.). Atlanta, GA: Bard Press.

Sprenger, M. (2003). *Differentiation through learning styles and memory.* Thousand Oaks, CA: Corwin Press.

Tool 12. Cycles of Concentration

Baddeley, A. (2004). *Your memory: A user's guide.* London: Carlton Books.

Brewer, C., & Campbell, D. (1991). *Rhythms of learning.* Tucson, AZ: Zephyr Press.

Howard, P. (2000). *The owner's manual for the brain* (2nd ed.). Atlanta, GA: Bard Press.

Jensen, E. (2006). *Enrich the brain.* Jossey-Bass. San Francisco.

Schacter, D. (1996). *Searching for memory: The brain, mind and the past.* London: Basic Books.

Smith, A. (2004). *The brain's behind it.* Stafford, UK: Network Educational Press.

Tool 13. State-Changes

Allen, R. (2002). *Impact teaching.* Boston: Allyn & Bacon.

Jensen, E. (2005). *Teaching with the brain in mind* (2nd ed.). Alexandra, VA: Association for Supervision and Curriculum Development.

Robbins, A. (1996). *Personal power 11.* San Diego, CA: Robins Research International.

Tool 14. Crossovers

Calvin, W. (1996). *How brains think.* London: Basic Books.

Cohen, I., & Goldsmith, M. (2002). *Hands on.* Ventura, CA: Edu-Kinesthetics.

Hannaford, C. (1993). *Education in motion* [video]. Tucson, AZ: Zephyr Press.

Hannaford, C. (1995). *Smart moves.* Arlington, VA: Great Ocean.

Robbins, A. (1996). *Personal power 11.* San Diego, CA: Robins Research International.

Tool 15. Improving Memory Links

Brain Store. (2002). *Adrenaline to go* [CD]. Thousand Oaks, CA: Sage.

Dispenza, J. (2007). *Evolve the brain.* Deerfield Beach, FL: Health Communications.

Gazzaniga, M. (2001). *Foundations in social neuroscience.* Cambridge, MA: MIT Press.

Jensen, E. (2005). *Teaching with the brain in mind* (2nd ed.). Alexandra, VA: Association for Supervision and Curriculum Development.

Prashnig, B. (1998). *The power of diversity.* Auckland, New Zealand: David Bateman.

Smith, A., Lovatt, M., & Wise, D (2003). *Accelerated learning: A user's guide.* Stafford, United Kingdom: Network Educational Press.

Sousa, D. (2005). *How the brain learns to read.* Thousand Oaks, CA: Corwin Press.

Sprenger, M. (2003). *Differentiation through learning styles and memory.* Thousand Oaks, CA: Corwin Press.

Tate, M. (2007). *Shouting won't grow dendrites.* Thousand Oaks, CA: Corwin Press.

Tool 16. Memory Techniques

Sprenger, M. (2003). *Differentiation through learning styles and memory.* Thousand Oaks, CA: Corwin Press.

Trudeau, K. (1997). *Mega memory.* Niles, IL: Nightingale Conant.

Tool 17. Rough Draft

Kovalik, S. (1997). *ITI: The model. Integrated thematic education.* Kent, WA: Susan Kovalik and Associates.

Prashnig, B. (1998). *The power of diversity.* Auckland, New Zealand: David Bateman.

Sprenger, M. (2003). *Differentiation through learning styles and memory.* Thousand Oaks, CA: Corwin Press.

Tool 18. Elaboration

Buzan, T. (1997). *The mindmap book.* London: BBC Books.

deBono, E. (1995). *Teach yourself to think.* London: Penguin Books.

Dispenza, J. (2007). *Evolve the brain.* Deerfield Beach, FL: Health Communications.

Frangenheim, E. (1998). *Reflections on classroom thinking strategies.* Loganholme, Australia: Rodin Educational Consultancy.

Gelb, M. (1995). *Thinking for a change.* London: Aurum Press.

Kovalik, S. (1997). *ITI: The model. Integrated thematic education.* Kent, WA: Susan Kovalik and Associates.

Raffini, J. (1996). *150 ways to increase intrinsic motivation in the classroom.* Boston: Allyn & Bacon.

Smith, A. (2004). *The brain's behind it.* Stafford, United Kingdom: Network Educational Press.

Tate, M. (2004). *"Sit and get" won't grow dendrites.* Thousand Oaks, CA: Corwin Press.

Trudeau, K. (1997). *Mega memory.* CITY: Nightingale Conant.

Tool 19. Repetition

Howard, P. (2000). *The owner's manual for the brain* (2nd ed.). Atlanta, GA: Bard Press.

Kovalik, S. (1997). *ITI: The model. Integrated thematic education.* Kent, WA: Susan Kovalik and Associates.

Sousa, D. (2005). *How the brain learns to read.* Thousand Oaks, CA: Corwin Press.

Sprenger, M. (2003). *Differentiation through learning styles and memory.* Thousand Oaks, CA: Corwin Press.

Udall, A. (1997). *Big questions, big ideas.* Tucson, AZ: Zephyr Press.

Tool 20. Themes

Kovalik, S. (1997). *ITI: The model. Integrated thematic education.* Kent, WA: Susan Kovalik and Associates.

Robbins, A. (1991). *Awaken the giant within.* Fireside: New York.

Udall, A. (1997). *Big questions, big ideas.* Tucson, AZ: Zephyr Press.

Part III. A Model for a "Learn to Learn" Framework

Burns, S. (1993). *Great lies we live by.* Ultimo, Australia: Caminole Pty.

Costa, A., & Kallick, B. (2000). *Activating and engaging habits of mind.* Alexandria, VA: Association for Supervision and Curriculum Development.

Gordon, N. (1995). *Magical classroom.* Tuscson, AZ: Zephyr Press.

Harmin, M. (1998). *Strategies to inspire active learning.* Edwardsville, IL: Inspiring Strategy Institute.

Jensen, E. (2006). *Enriching the brain.* San Francisco: Jossey-Bass.

Prashnig, B. (1996). *Diversity is our strength.* Auckland, New Zealand: Profile Books.

Prashnig, B. (1998). *The power of diversity.* Auckland, New Zealand: David Bateman.

Scaddan M. (2002). *Twenty rules of the game of school.* Tauranga, New Zealand: Brain Stems.

Tool 21. Input Through Learning Styles

Dunn, R., & Dunn, K. (1994). *Teaching elementary students through their individual learning styles, grade 3–6.* Boston: Allyn & Bacon.

Jensen, E. (2006). *Enriching the brain.* San Francisco: Jossey-Bass.

Prashnig, B. (1996). *Diversity is our strength.* Auckland, New Zealand: Profile Books.

Sprenger, M. (2003). *Differentiation through learning styles and memory.* Thousand Oaks, CA: Corwin Press.

Tool 22. Learning Preferences

Dryden, G., & Voss, J. (2001). *The learning revolution.* Auckland, New Zealand: The Learning Web.

Dunn, R., & Dunn, K. (1994). *Teaching elementary students through their individual learning styles, grade 3–6.* Boston: Allyn & Bacon.

Ginnis, P. (2002). *The teacher's toolkit.* Bancyfelin, United Kingdom: Crown House.

Jensen, E. (2005). *Teaching with the brain in mind* (2nd ed.). Alexandra, VA: Association for Supervision and Curriculum Development.

Miles, E. (1997). *Tune your brain.* New York: Berkley.

Tool 23. Multiple Intelligences

Buzan, T. (2000). *Head first.* London: Thorsons.

Dryden, G., & Voss, J. (2001). *The learning revolution.* Auckland, New Zealand: The Learning Web.

Gardner, H. (1983). *Frames of mind.* New York: Basic Books.

Gardner, H. (1999). *Intelligence reframed.* New York: Basic Books.

Goleman, D. (1996). *Emotional intelligence.* London: Bloomsbury.

Goleman, D. (2006). *Social intelligence.* London: Random House.

Jensen, E. (2006). *Enriching the brain.* San Francisco: Jossey-Bass.

Pink, D. (2003). *A whole new mind.* Crows Nest, Australia: Allen & Unwin.

Tool 24. Motivators

Canfield, J. (2005). *The success principles.* London: Element.

Glasser, W. (1998). *Choice theory.* New York: Harper Perennial.

Kraus, S. (2002). *Psychological foundations of success.* San Francisco: Change Planet Press.

Raffini, J. (1996). *150 ways to increase intrinsic motivation in the classroom.* Boston: Allyn & Bacon.

Reiss, S. (2000). *Who am I?* New York: Berkley Books.

Robbins, A. (1996). *Personal power 11.* San Diego, CA: Robins Research International.

Rogers, S. (2003). *Key connections: The brain, motivation and achievement.* San Diego, CA: The Brain Store.

Scaddan M. (2002). *Twenty rules of the game of school.* Tauranga, New Zealand: Brain Stems.

Smith, A. (2004). *The brain's behind it.* Stafford, United Kingdom: Network Educational Press.

Tool 25. Four Great Questions

Glasser, W. (1998). *Choice theory.* New York: Harper Perennial.

Kraus, S. (2002). *Psychological foundations of success.* San Francisco: Change Planet Press.

Robbins, A. (1996). *Personal power 11.* San Diego, CA: Robins Research International.

Tool 26. WIIFM

Canfield, J. (2005). *The success principles.* London: Element.

Frankl, V. (2004). *Man's search for meaning.* Sydney, Australia: Random House.

Ginnis, P. (2002). *The teacher's toolkit.* Bancyfelin, United Kingdom: Crown House.

Harmin, M. (1998). *Strategies to inspire active learning.* Edwardsville, IL: Inspiring Strategy Institute.
Pinker, S. (1997). *How the mind works.* New York: W. W. Norton.
Politano, C., & Paquin, J. (2000). *Brain-based learning with class.* Winnipeg, Canada: Portage & Main Press.
Rogers, S. (2003). *Key connections: The brain, motivation and achievement.* San Diego, CA: The Brain Store.
Rose, C., & Nicholl, M. (1997). *Accelerated learning for the 21st century.* New York: Piatkus.

Tool 27. Pulling Your Own Strings

Dyer, W. (1977). *Pulling your own strings.* New York: Avon Books.
Robbins, A. (1996). *Personal power 11.* San Diego, CA: Robins Research International.

Tool 28. Goal Setting

Buzan, T. (2001). *Head strong.* London: Thorsons.
Canfield, J. (2005). *The success principles.* London: Element.
Canfield, J., & Hansen, M. V. (2000). *The power of focus.* London: Vermillion.
Covey, S. (2004). *The 8th habit.* London: Simon & Schuster.
Frankl, V. (2004). *Man's search for meaning.* Sydney, Australia: Random House.
Kraus, S. (2002). *Psychological foundations of success.* San Francisco: Change Planet Press.
Secunda, A. (1999). *The 15-second principle.* New York: Berkeley.

Tool 29. "Myffirmations"

Buzan, T. (2001). *Head strong.* London: Thorsons.
Canfield, J., & Hansen, M. V. (2003). *Chicken soup for the soul: Living your dreams.* Deerfield Beach, FL: Health Communications.
DePorter, B. (1992). *Quantum learning.* London: Piatkus.
Dryden, G., & Voss, J. (2001). *The learning revolution.* Auckland, New Zealand: The Learning Web.
Dyer, W. (2004). *The power of intention.* Carlsbad, CA: Hay House.
Kaufeldt, M. (2001). *Begin with the brain.* Thousand Oaks, CA: Corwin Press.
Kehoe, J. (1998). *Mind power into the 21st century.* Vancouver, Canada: Zoetic.
Parker, J. (1993). *Build a winning self-image.* Vancouver, Canada: Gateway Research Institute.
Sapolsky, R. (1998). *Why zebras don't get ulcers.* New York: W. H. Freeman.

Tool 30. Overviews

Allen, R. (2002). *Impact learning.* Boston: Allyn & Bacon.
Blanchard, K., & Johnson, S. (1996). *The one-minute manager.* London: Harper Collins.
Buzan, T. (2001). *Head strong.* London: Thorsons.
Fogarty, R. (2002). *Brain compatible classrooms.* Thousand Oaks, CA: Corwin Press.
Jensen, E. (2005). *Teaching with the brain in mind* (2nd ed.). Alexandra, VA: Association for Supervision and Curriculum Development.
Kaufeldt, M. (2001). *Begin with the brain.* Thousand Oaks, CA: Corwin Press.
Prashnig, B. (1998). *The power of diversity.* Auckland, New Zealand: David Bateman.

Raffini, J. (1996). *150 ways to increase intrinsic motivation in the classroom.* Boston: Allyn & Bacon.
Smith, A. (2004). *The brain's behind it.* London: Network Educational Press.

Tool 31. Framing

Allen, R. (2001). *Train smart.* Thousand Oaks, CA: Corwin Press.
Allen, R. (2002). *Impact teaching.* Boston: Allyn & Bacon.
Barrett, S. (1992). *It's all in your head . . .* Minneapolis, MN: Free Spirit.
Jensen, E. (2006). *Enriching the brain.* San Francisco: Jossey-Bass.

Tool 32. Prewiring

Allen, R. (2001). *Train smart.* Thousand Oaks, CA: Corwin Press.
Allen, R. (2002). *Impact teaching.* Boston: Allyn & Bacon.
Carter, R. (1998). *Mapping the mind.* London: Weidenfield & Nicholson.
DePorter, B., Reardon, M., & Singer-Nourie, S. (1999). *Quantum teaching.* Boston: Allyn & Bacon.
Howard, P. (2000). *The owner's manual for the brain* (2nd ed.). Atlanta, GA: Bard Press.
Smith, A. (2004). *The brain's behind it.* London: Network Educational Press.
Tate, M. (2004) *"Sit and get" won't grow dendrites.* Thousand Oaks, CA: Corwin Press.

Tool 33. Loops

Allen, R. (2001). *Train smart.* Thousand Oaks, CA: Corwin Press.
Allen, R. (2002). *Impact learning.* Boston: Allyn & Bacon.
Barrett, S. (1992*). It's all in your head . . .* Minneapolis, MN: Free Spirit.
Dispenza, J. (2007). *Evolve the brain.* Deerfield Beach, FL: Health Communications.

Tool 34. Feedback

deBono, E. (1995). *Teach yourself to think.* London: Penguin Books.
Chernow, F. (1997). *The sharper mind.* Paramus, NJ: Prentice Hall.
Gelb, M. (1995). *Thinking for a change.* London: Aurum Press.
Harmin, M. (1998). *Strategies to inspire active learning.* Edwardsville, IL: Inspiring Strategy Institute.
Jensen, E. (2005). *Teaching with the brain in mind* (2nd ed.). Alexandra, VA: Association for Supervision and Curriculum Development.
Jensen, E. (2006). *Enriching the brain.* San Francisco: Jossey-Bass.
Kaufeldt, M. (2001). *Begin with the brain.* Thousand Oaks, CA: Corwin Press.

Tool 35. Mind Maps and Mindscapes

Buzan, T. (1997). *The mindmap book.* London: BBC Books.
Gelb, M. (1995). *Thinking for a change.* London: Aurum Press.
Marguiles, N. (1992). *Mapping inner space.* Heatherton, Australia: Hawker Brownlow Education.

Tool 36. Reflection

Canfield, J. (2005). *The success principles.* London: Element.
deBono, E. (1994). *Parallel thinking.* London: Penguin Books.

deBono, E. (1995). *Teach yourself to think.* London: Penguin Books.

Kovalik, S. (1997). *ITI: The model. Integrated thematic education.* Kent, WA: Susan Kovalik and Associates.

Kraus, S. (2002). *Psychological foundations of success.* San Francisco: Change Planet Press.

Scaddan, M. (2002). *Twenty rules of the game of school.* Tauranga, New Zealand: Brain Stems.

Udall, A., & Daniels, J. (1991). *Creating the thoughtful classroom.* Tucson, AZ: Zephyr Press.

Tool 37. Lo, Mo, and Ho Questions

Allen, R. (2002). *Impact learning.* Boston: Allyn & Bacon.

Costa, A. (2000). *Discovering and exploring habits of mind.* Alexandra, VA: Association for Supervision and Curriculum Development.

Fogarty, R. (2002). *Brain compatible classrooms.* Arlington Heights, IL: Thousand Oaks, CA: Corwin Press.

Frangenheim, E. (1998). *Reflections on classroom thinking strategies.* Loganholme, Australia: Rodin Educational Consultancy.

Katterns, B. (April 2002). *Accessing higher level thinking through better questions.* Workshop at Te Puna School, Tauranga, New Zealand.

Sternberg, R., & Grigorenko, E. (2000). *Teaching for successful intelligence* (2nd ed.). Thousand Oaks, CA: Corwin Press.

Udall, A. (1997). *Big questions, big ideas.* Tucson, AZ: Zephyr Press.

Tool 38. Inclusive Responses

Allen, R. (2002). *Impact learning.* Boston: Allyn & Bacon.

Fogarty, R. (2002). *Brain compatible classrooms.* Thousand Oaks, CA: Corwin Press.

Rief, S., & Heimburge, J. (1996). *How to reach & teach all children in the inclusive classroom.* New York: The Center for Applied Research in Education.

Tool 39. Response Time

Allen, R. (2002*). Impact learning.* Boston: Allyn & Bacon.

Bloom B. S. (1956). *Taxonomy of educational objectives, Handbook I: The cognitive domain.* New York: David McKay.

Fogarty, R. (2002). *Brain compatible classrooms.* Thousand Oaks, CA: Corwin Press.

Katterns, B. (April 2002). *Accessing higher level thinking through better questions.* Workshop at Te Puna School, Tauranga, New Zealand.

Tool 40. Hands-Free: An Obligation to Answer

Allen, R. (2002). *Impact teaching.* Boston: Allyn & Bacon.

deBono, E. (1995). *Teach yourself to think.* London: Penguin Books.

Raffini, J. (1996). *150 ways to increase intrinsic motivation in the classroom.* Boston: Allyn & Bacon.

Rief, S., & Heimburge, J. (1996). *How to reach & teach all children in the inclusive classroom.* New York The Center For Applied Research in Education.

Scaddan, M. (2002). *Twenty rules of the game of school.* Tauranga, New Zealand: Brain Stems.

Index

CORWIN PRESS

The Corwin Press logo—a raven striding across an open book—represents the union of courage and learning. Corwin Press is committed to improving education for all learners by publishing books and other professional development resources for those serving the field of PreK–12 education. By providing practical, hands-on materials, Corwin Press continues to carry out the promise of its motto: **"Helping Educators Do Their Work Better."**